Drama and Movement in Therapy

DRAMA AND MOVEMENT IN THERAPY

The Therapeutic Use of Movement, Drama and Music

AUDREY G. WETHERED, L.R.A.M.

Trained in the Laban Art of Movement and tutor for "Sesame"

MACDONALD & EVANS LTD
8 John Street, London WC1N 2HY
1973

First published June 1973

©

MACDONALD AND EVANS LIMITED

1973

ISBN: 0 7121 0411 9

Printed in Great Britain by Unwin Brothers Limited
The Gresham Press, Old Woking, Surrey, England
A member of the Staples Printing Group

Preface

THERE is at present a dearth of literature about movement and drama in therapy, and as yet there is no recognised training for a movement therapist, on a par with physiotherapy or occupational therapy.

However, interest has been growing and students can choose Movement, Dance or Drama Therapy as a subject for theses, essays or research. Many people both in education and medicine are finding that they have a beneficial effect, and some have come to realise that all the arts can have a deep effect on psychic processes, particularly in conjunction with psycho-therapy, and need handling with great care.

Originally I trained at the Royal Academy of Music, and as a nurse during and after the Second World War I began to understand something of how to relate to patients and to see the part the arts might play in healing. Pursuing the possibility of music being practised therapeutically, I became aware from the reaction of patients of the need for active participation. I studied several forms of movement and dance and finally took part in the Laban Art of Movement, which led to a training when I was privileged to study individually with Rudolf Laban.

Here I found a man who, though accepting one as one was, opened up enormous possibilities, for he had a deep under-standing of people. He was genial, wise, a man of vision, yet one who could stimulate and guide people to discover, create and develop for themselves. His study of painting, sculpture, architecture, stage design and theatrical production led him ultimately to the observation and study of movement and dance; he was insistent that his was not a method, system or technique but rather a way of working based on the principles underlying all movement which could be applied in every walk of life—the arts, industry, education, drama, the stage, in therapy and in daily living. Latterly he became concerned with the links between movement and the development of personality.

In this book, I have attempted to write for those experienced in therapy who desire to understand movement, for those trained in movement who seek to apply their knowledge in remedial and therapeutic fields, and as an introduction to both movement and therapy for those from other disciplines.

I have particularly stressed the principles of movement, as I have found these invaluable guidelines, but I have drawn from many sources including my own invention, imagination and observation, for in therapy one can have no fixed ideas. Every time one meets a patient a new situation arises which demands assessment, and demands that one draw on one's own resources in order to relate and adapt.

With examples from my own work, I have tried to show how it is possible to apply one's knowledge. Though for convenience I have separated movement and drama, I find them inter-related, for one is inherent in the other. I have also touched on relaxation, for in this age of stress we need to find ways of using our energies with as little strain as possible, as well as to take time to "let go," relax and rest.

Relationship, to me, is all-important also, for where there is no relatedness between the one in need and the one guiding there can be no healing.

Finally, I have devoted a section to music, as it plays such a large part in therapeutic work.

In the text I have used the word "he" in a general way, but often it could equally well be "she."

I hope the reader will bear with me if he finds repetition. Years ago, an elderly Dutchman said to me: "Learning comes through repetition." I believe some things need such stress.

Acknowledgments

I AM grateful to all those who have made the writing of this book possible, especially Dr. A. I. Allenby.

I am indebted to those who have given me the encouragement, support and advice in my work that has enabled me to undertake this task, also to those who have helped me in the preparation of the manuscript, giving me most helpful comments. Among these, I would particularly like to thank Dr. A. I. Allenby, Miss Chloë Gardner, Mrs. Monk Gibbon, Mr. John Hudson, Mrs. Marian Lindkvist, Dr. Joan Mackworth and Mr. Peter Slade.

My thanks are also due to the following authors and publishers for permission to quote from their books:

Mr. Peter Slade and Longmans for the extract from *Experience of Spontaneity*. Routledge and Kegan Paul for the extract from *Modern Man in Search of a Soul*, by C. G. Jung.

The Orthological Institute for the extracts from *The Image and Appearance of the Human Body*, by Paul Schilder, M.D., Ph.D.

Theatre Arts Books (New York) for permission to reprint the extract from *Stanislavski's Legacy*.

I would also like to thank all the patients for the privilege of working with them, without whom I could never have begun.

Introduction

THE common denominator of all human activity is, in fact, movement. Even in stillness, heartbeat and breathing continue, and the qualities of movement can be recognised in facial expression and body attitude, for example, the intensity or living quality that an actor or dancer radiates throughout a pause, so that continuity is not broken and there is no hiatus in the action.

Because patients are inhibited in using their bodies as their expressive and communicating instruments by reason of their mental or psychological state, it is imperative never to lose sight of the whole person, from whatever angle one approaches work with him. For convenience, we make a dichotomy of the inner and the outer, and sometimes we shall be concerned with one, sometimes with the other; but both are aspects of the whole rather than two separate entities.

When holding a ball in the hand and turning it around, there is always one point of the surface which is nearest to one's face, and in considering movement or drama there are different principles, aspects, ways of approach. Sometimes one will be more stressed, sometimes another, but a continuum is there as well. Drama, however, has distinct techniques, as we see in voice production, speech and acting.

Breaking down the whole into parts may give the therapist or teacher more insight, but it is for him to translate the work into a form or vocabulary which he can transmit to those with whom he is working. A doctor has to study physiology, anatomy, chemistry, pathology, psychology and how the body and mind function; but when he comes to treat the patient, it is in a human relationship and the patient does not need to go into all the details that the doctor understands. In the same way, the therapist needs to break down his art, observe, learn and understand it and then use it as a whole, usually in an indirect way. Through participating in the art, there can be a dawning awareness or consciousness.

Occasionally one meets patients who can use the material they have created or experienced in music, drama, art or dance for their own self-discovery, so it is also necessary for the therapist or teacher to understand something of himself, how he functions in body, mind, imagination and feeling.

WHAT IS THERAPY?

Therapy is a term very loosely used these days, and there is no distinct dividing line to distinguish it from remedial or specialised education. This leads to a certain confusion.

The derivation of the word is from the Greek verb *"therapeuin"* (to take care of, to heal) and the noun *"therapeia"* (service, treatment), which is probably the reason why the medical profession has taken it in the specific meaning of "treatment" and "healing." Then the word "heal" has various derivations, all meaning "whole," so it may be here that the confusion has arisen. Not one of us is really "whole," we all need help to find and fulfil ourselves. More and more it is being recognised how great a part education needs to play in such development, particularly now that there has to be provision for so many handicapped children in special schools for the educationally sub-normal, the maladjusted and the physically and mentally handicapped. Obviously these children benefit enormously from remedial and specialised teaching, and in that sense it can be considered therapeutic.

Yet "therapy" is used specifically in the sense of "treatment" of illness or disease, and so we get electro-convulsive therapy, occupational therapy, physiotherapy, psychotherapy, radio-therapy, and so on. These are prescribed by a doctor and are undertaken by trained doctors, nurses, and therapists covering all departments of hospitals, clinics and domiciliary services, and to practise any of these therapies appropriate training, experience and qualifications are required.

Now that the arts have entered the medical world in the form of music therapy and art therapy the problem of "what is therapy?" becomes more complex.

THE ROLE OF THE THERAPIST

The ideal practitioner is one who, in addition to a knowledge of pathology, has not only acquired particular techniques and skill in therapy but also has a flair for understanding and handling patients, which enables him to create the atmosphere and conditions in which the patient can co-operate and benefit fully from the particular discipline and in which the mysterious process we call healing can take place.

Some therapists have the skill and knowledge without this flair, and some people who are trained only in their art have this flair but have not the medical knowledge, yet call themselves "therapists."

The therapist's integrity depends on his working within the limits of his discipline, and he needs training in the understanding of the illness he is treating, the aims and techniques of treatment and his role in the treatment team.

Training is some check on who is allowed to tend patients and is a safeguard for the patient, for there are those who may want to use their art in the medical field simply because they have found no other opening, and not because they are primarily concerned with the need of patients. Some whose lives are emotionally disturbed are attracted to therapeutic work because of their own need; if they can sort out their own problems before they attempt to help patients they can often do very valuable work.

The fact that they have suffered and worked to come to terms with their own experience has turned it into an asset. By gaining understanding of themselves they are aware of other people's difficulties and are alive to the danger of projecting their own difficulties on to patients or of caring for others in order to compensate for the lack of care in their own lives.

For these reasons there should be some standard, which need not be so rigid that the situation arises where someone who has given highly-praised and satisfactory service for years is ousted, simply because he has never undertaken a particular training.

At the time of writing, there is much concern over and interest in the arts in medicine, and already attempts are being made to provide some training for those who want to use the arts in therapy. Let us hope that eventually we may have a training in the arts which is recognised; it is, after all, not so very long ago that occupational therapy was taught because it was "nice for patients to occupy themselves with a little knitting or basketry." Now it is being realised how much more there can be to it than that.

However, the inclusion of the arts in the overall programme of treatment, as distinct from their use as remedial education or as a diversion, will mean a proliferation of therapies, so there is a danger that unless those undertaking them are fully trained both to apply their art and take their place in the treatment team, these therapies will not be taken seriously by the medical profession.

Contents

Preface   v

Acknowledgments   vii

Introduction   ix

List of Illustrations   xvi

CHAP.

PART ONE: MOVEMENT

I Principles of Movement

    What we move   4
    Where we move   5
    How we move   9
    Qualities of movement   10
    Basic actions   12

II Movement Work With Patients

    How to handle a session   17
    Preparation of work   17
    Preparation of the body for action   17

III Movement Themes and Sequences as Starting-points

    Developing a theme   23
    The build-up   25

IV Specific Ways of Using Movement in Therapy

    Play—its importance in personal development   31
    Lack of play in childhood   33
    How play and make-believe can be explored and experienced by adults   34
    Space—used as a progression towards greater awareness   36

Use of objects to emphasise external reality   38
Coming to terms with aggression   40
Fantasy unrelated to life   46
The relationship of body-image, body aware-   50
     ness and imagination
The piano used to develop relationship to   51
     the outer world
Use of music   53
Conclusions   57

PART TWO: DRAMA

V   The Use of Drama in Therapy
Playing a role   61
Variety of ability   62
Improvisation   63
Writing a play   64
Play-reading   64
Producing a play   64

VI   Drama Group at "Holyrood," South Leigh
Introduction   66
Impromptu acting   67
Characterisation   68
Stimulating the invention of character   69

VII   Mime and Speech
Mime   71
Speech   74
Sentences   76
Plays   76
Role-playing   77

VIII   Pilot Study for a Research Project undertaken
     by "Sesame"
Introduction   79
Formation of the group   80
How the drama group was used   80
The general work of the patients   81
Themes and scenes used   83

Contents

PART THREE: RELAXATION AND RELATIONSHIP

IX   Relaxation

    The function of relaxation   91
    How tensions arise   94
    Realisation of tension and ways of release   95

 X   Relationship

    Importance of relationship   100
    Training awareness between partners   101
    Qualities needed for work with patients   102
    Themes to develop trust and confidence   103
    Groups and how to use them   108

PART FOUR: MUSIC

XI   Response to Music

    Recorded music   113
    Choice of music   114
    The importance of listening in choosing   115
      music

XII   Music as Therapy

    Consideration of group preferences   119
    The use of voice   121

Appendixes

  I   General list of useful musical pieces   122

 II   Bibliography   125

Index   127

List of Illustrations

FIG.

1. Body awareness   5
2. Body shape   6
3. Forwards   7
4. Light and sudden   10
5. Direct and flexible   11
6. Is the water hot or cold?   14
7. Body parts meeting   24
8. Crawling   35
9. Feeling an object   39
10. Flinging a cushion   42
11. Pitting strength   43
12. Leading with an elbow   47
13. The fantasy pattern   48
14. Playing with a feather   73
15. Bursting in   75
16. Doing homage   84
17. Holding a baby   86
18. Sitting at a desk   92
19. Stretching   93
20. Taking a partner's weight   104
21. Allowing oneself to be overcome   105
22. Leading and following   106
23. Playing with hands   107

Part One

MOVEMENT

CHAPTER I

Principles of Movement

BEFORE attempting to explore the application of movement or drama in therapy, it is necessary to know the basic principles that underlie all movement, whether purely bodily activity, or purposeful action, or movement in an expressive form, or in communication. We cannot live without moving, for we breathe continually, we cannot see, sing, speak or act, pursue work or sport, or convey what is within us of thought, feeling, imagination or passion without moving.

Movement is a continuum. The body is the instrument, it moves indoors and outdoors, bending, stretching, turning and twisting with a variety of efforts and qualities which convey the particular character and temperament of the person who moves, or the character he is attempting to portray, and in turn enables him to relate and adapt to other people either in ordinary life or in make-believe.

When taking one aspect of movement in order to clarify what we are seeing or doing or experiencing, we need to be constantly aware of the other factors: if we use a finger to play a note on the piano, we may be concentrating on the smooth pathway made by that finger, and the amount of energy we are using. We also need to be aware that not only is the whole body involved, but that there is thought and feeling, sensation and imagination behind even that small action, otherwise the hands could only be used mechanically.

These principles of movement can be divided into four main categories:

1. *What we move*

The body—as a whole, its different parts in isolation and

3

co-ordination and the shapes taken by the body in the course of moving.

2. *Where we move*

The space—that immediately around us into which we can reach—personal space—the space in which we find ourselves, the room, hall, etc. in which we move—general space.

3. *How we move*

The quality of movement—the dynamics or efforts which convey our inner selves, express ourselves, and achieve our actions.

4. *With whom we move*

Relationship—the world of people with whom we live and work and play.

WHAT WE MOVE

1. *Body awareness*

In order to have command over our bodies, we need to become aware of them as a whole, and of the different parts in isolation and co-ordination (*see* Fig. 1).

2. *Symmetry*

We can move both sides of the body simultaneously or only one side at a time.

3. *Shape*

The body has a natural capacity to stretch, bend, turn and twist, bringing it into varying attitudes which can be flat, rounded or pointed (*see* Fig. 2).

For instance, to accept a cup of tea, the arm has to be extended, the cup taken in the hand, the fingers grasping the handle. Then the cup has to be raised to the lips by the co-ordination of all these parts before the tea can be drunk. The different parts—shoulder, arm, fingers, mouth—come into play without our consciously thinking of them, because from infancy we have used and explored and developed our

4

Fig. 1   Body awareness: parts in co-ordination

bodies so that we can make successive actions of approaching, grasping, handling and setting down quite instinctively.

To pick up a bundle of washing, both arms are needed, both legs balance and support, and the whole body is involved in the action of lifting.

WHERE WE MOVE

Whether in personal or general space, we move at different levels and in different directions.

1. *Levels*

These can be HIGH, MEDIUM, and DEEP. When arms and legs are used in gesture, the level is according to the joint from which the movement is activated. At medium level, the leg would be used at hip level, high when it is above, and deep when it is below the hip. The same applies to the arm in relation to the shoulder. Stepping would be high when on

5

Fig. 2   Round and flat body shapes

the toes, medium with the whole foot, and deep with bent knees.

It is also possible to move high with the intention deep, *i.e.* towards the ground, or deep with the intention high, *i.e.* upwards.

2. *Directions*

These are:

FORWARD

LEFT   RIGHT

BACKWARD

If we add the levels to these high and deep directions, we get dimensions:

3. *Dimensions* (*see* Fig. 3)

HIGH	DEEP
RIGHT	LEFT
BACKWARD	FORWARD

Fig. 3   Dimensions: forwards

4. *Diagonals*

LEFT FORWARD	RIGHT BACKWARD
LEFT BACKWARD	RIGHT FORWARD

Again adding the levels, high and deep, we get:

LEFT FORWARD HIGH to RIGHT BACKWARD DEEP
LEFT BACKWARD HIGH to RIGHT FORWARD DEEP
LEFT FORWARD DEEP to RIGHT BACKWARD HIGH
LEFT BACKWARD HIGH to RIGHT FORWARD DEEP

and vice-versa.

In one session, I used the dimensions as my starting-point. I suggested that each patient should imagine he was inside a cube, which he was to explore. They all responded very well, feeling imaginary walls, ceiling and floor, going towards and away from the limits they had set themselves in their cube. Some used the corners, so that in fact they experimented with

7

diagonals. I don't remember now if I used the word "dimension," it would have been quite unnecessary if I did.

The qualities that emerged were on the whole rather straight and controlled, so quite suddenly I changed the theme to get contrast, *e.g.* flexibility, and said: "Now you are in a plastic bag, see if you can get out of it." That had been the only time so far that I had used this idea. Immediately I was asked: "Can we have our heads out?" Realising I had unexpectedly touched on a problem, I naturally agreed. At such moments one is tempted to think: "What have I done? Why did I ask for this? What will happen?" When such a situation arises quite spontaneously and without any premeditation, provided one is aware that there is a difficulty, pays attention and is ready to help if needed, one can risk letting a patient explore, experience and try to find his own limits.

When we came to an end, the person concerned looked amazed and said: "I would never have believed Audrey could have got me to do that, you see I was born with a caul over my head, and believing I was already dead the doctor and midwife put me at the foot of my mother's bed and turned their attention to her. Only when they had finished did the midwife discover I was still breathing. I have always suffered from asphyxia."

Now I knew nothing of all this, and indeed had I known would have avoided suggesting anything so claustrophobic as a plastic bag. Yet a traumatic experience relived in the presence of a therapist can be of value, because it is in a controlled situation.

In moving at different levels and in different directions we expand and contract, we become narrow or wide with varying degrees of expansion. So we can say we move from small to large, and from near to far.

If we experiment in our own personal space, we can move either closed in near to our bodies or extended away from our bodies. Our intention can be the same as our movement, or it can be the opposite. We can move near to ourselves, and yet be concerned with what is beyond ourselves, or we can be extended away from ourselves and yet be concerned with our own person.

If we experiment in general space our expansion can take us

over the floor, opening out; or retreating, we can close in towards ourselves.

5. *Pathways*

Our bodies can move in a straight, angular or twisted way in our own personal space creating different patterns, whether the whole body or gestures of arms or legs are used. These pathways are then in the air around us. In general space, moving over the floor, we also use straight, angular and curved pathways, which create floor pattern.

One way of using the idea of pathways is to ask people to step the shape of a figure or letter, *e.g.* the initials of their Christian names.

HOW WE MOVE

We each have a distinct, unique personality, call it mind, spirit, soul, psyche, what you will. Without this inner life the body cannot function, as it needs the activation of thought, emotion, feeling, sensation, instinct or intuition in order to be put in motion. This causes us to move in particular ways, which express what we are in our inner selves, and we are able to recognise people, and sense their moods or states by their movement, even if we cannot see their features. Before I ever studied movement, I had two experiences which illustrate this.

When lunching with friends, I met a doctor. The following day, I was walking through the garden of the home in which she was working. As I neared the window I saw a pair of hands folding a table napkin, and immediately knew they were hers. Sure enough, this was proved correct when she came into full view. Yet, had I been asked, I would have said I had never looked at her hands, let alone seen how she used them.

On another occasion, I was with a friend in a picture gallery, and we noticed a lady who seemed familiar, yet we were neither of us sure. After we had followed her for some time she suddenly made a gesture, and without thinking I exclaimed: "Mrs. So-and-so always moved like that!" It was twenty years since we had last met, but this gesture made me so sure that I went up and spoke to her, and only then did I realise that

I must have registered this type of movement quite unconsciously, as being especially her own.

All of us, whether consciously or unconsciously are affected by expressive movement, and tone of voice. The actor instinctively observes people, when we watch dancers or actors, we respond to their art in conveying what they intend, and the greater the artist the fuller our participation in the experience. The same is true in a slightly different way of musicians, performers or conductors. Even listening to music over the radio or on record without any visual contact, we are still aware of the qualities produced by the playing of the musical instrument or the use of the voice.

QUALITIES OF MOVEMENT

It is these qualities of movement (*see* Figs. 4 and 5) that

Fig. 4   Qualities: light and sudden

Fig. 5 Qualities: direct and flexible

convey what we have to contribute, and how we communicate.

Again, for simplicity and to act as some guide, these qualities have been divided into four main categories: weight, energy or force, space, time and flow.

I am using the term "energy" in this context because it implies variation in intensity, "space" in the sense of how we move into space, as distinct from the space around us, and "flow" in the sense of continuity of movement.

These qualities can be sub-divided into elements:

Qualities	Elements
ENERGY	Strength, Lightness
SPACE	Direct, Flexible

11

Qualities	*Elements*	
TIME	Sudden,	Sustained
FLOW	Free,	Bound

The manner in which these movement elements inter-relate reveals the unique personality or character, and if we understand something about how these interchanges can affect other people, we can often find a way of relating to people who normally we find irritating, or difficult.

A man told me once that he had been dining with a friend and engaged in a most absorbing conversation; but when the band began to play a tune he knew, he turned suddenly to look at the players. With that unconscious movement the whole harmony of the evening was broken. Fortunately, he realised what had happened and so was able to re-establish the relationship.

Since patients are particularly sensitive to the movement of others, it behoves us to know something of how we express ourselves, to know how other people's ways of expression affect us, to acquire the ability to be aware of patients and sense their needs, and to develop the necessary concentration and attention so that we can react to the smallest changes in their moods and feelings and attempt to meet the needs these express.

Such observation is especially necessary with those patients who cannot verbalise, in order to make some relationship with them, for in movement, mime and drama one can often, simply through one's attitude, find a way of getting a response from them.

BASIC ACTIONS

In our actions, three qualities come into play: energy, space and time. Action has itself been divided into eight basic types. These have been arranged below so that in passing from one action to another only one element is changed, because this is the easiest way for people to experience these changes. Naturally, there are other ways of arranging these actions whilst still changing only one element, and it then becomes easier to change two elements and finally all three. The element changed in each case is italicised.

12

Actions	*Elements*
THRUST	Strength—directness and suddenness
PRESS	Strength—directness and *sustainment*
WRING	Strength—*flexibility* and sustainment
SLASH	Strength—flexibility and *suddenness*
FLICK	*Lightness*—flexibility and suddenness
DAB	Lightness—*directness* and suddenness
GLIDE	Lightness—directness and *sustainment*
FLOAT	Lightness—*flexibility* and sustainment

All these basic actions could be approached from the point of view of mime, and the following are just a few ideas.

THRUST	Hammering
	Swatting a fly with a fly-whisk
	Beating or punching someone
PRESS	Pulling on a rope
	Pushing away a heavy object
	Lifting a heavy load
WRING	Unscrewing a very stiff stopper
	Wringing out a floorcloth
SLASH	Slashing at a wasp that came too near
	Whipping a top
	Cracking a whip
FLICK	Flicking dust off clothes
	Flicking hair out of one's eyes
	Flicking away a tiny insect
DAB	Dabbing cotton wool on a sore place
	Patting one's face
	Testing water to see if it is cold (*see* Fig. 6)
GLIDE	Feeling a delicate smooth material
	Smoothing sand off a flat surface
FLOAT	Following the pathway of a feather or thistledown blown by the wind
	Disentangling a very fragile thread

Because I was concerned with students who could not invent or imagine, I experimented by devising a story of the building of Noah's Ark, founding it on basic actions and space. The following story evolved:

Noah's Ark

Noah has been told of the coming flood, and in order to build an ark to preserve his family he sends his sons into the forest to cut down trees to get the wood for building the ark.

WRING

SLASH

The sons make their way through clinging lianas, and have to slash their way through the undergrowth. All the time they are looking around them to decide

Fig. 6   Is the water hot or cold?

14

SPACE	which trees to fell. Having done so they set to work to hack the trees down, taking
THRUST	care to plan where each tree shall fall so
SPACE	as not to hurt anyone. The trees then have
PRESS GLIDE	to be sawn into planks, and smoothed and divided into suitable lengths. The wind
FLOAT	comes and blows the shavings about, but when ready the planks are dusted and
FLICK	polished. Clothes and hair are also dusty, and are flicked clean. By now, it is evening and mosquitoes and other small insects come out to torment the workers. They return to their camp and in the ensuing days bring the wood, dragging and pulling
PRESS	it to the place where they set to work to build the ark. Sometimes someone is
THRUST	unlucky and hammers his own hand,
DAB	which then has to be tended, but eventually the ark is built.

I found as I considered the different actions I got the ideas; for instance, pondering on wringing I saw the forest and lianas hanging down, and when thinking of space I felt the need to look around at how high the trees were, and whether there was room for the trees to fall. When the students came to act the story they took on the character of Noah and his family, and so the principle of relationship came in.

In all these qualities of movement there is increase and decrease. In looking, there are degrees from looking fixedly and intently to paying little attention. In speech, there are variations from a whisper to a shout or scream. If we want to move something we may start thinking it will be quite easy so do not exert our strength, but gradually we have to increase that strength until we can shift the object.

So in these qualities of energy, space and time there can be increase and decrease from strong to light, acceleration and deceleration between suddenness and sustainment, and there can be changes in the degrees of directness and flexibility. There can be increase and decrease in flow as well, from flowing so freely that one is taken off balance, to such holding back that the flow becomes bound.

These basic principles of movement I have found invaluable when working with patients; I do not necessarily use them as they stand, but they may stimulate my ideas, or give structure to what I plan. I have them to fall back on when I run out of ideas, or when I am faced with an unusual situation, or when I have to deal with emotional reactions.

CHAPTER II

Movement Work With Patients

HOW TO HANDLE A SESSION

FIRST and foremost, and in fact all the time, I work from what the patients give me, and to do this I must observe them—not in the sense of prying into their privacy, but to help them to extend their own capacities. For only a few can convey what they want in words, and if they can it may not be really what they need. So what I see in their movement helps me to sum up their capabilities and the mood they are in; from that, I can assess the approach I can use before deciding on the material to give them that they can use to develop and discover for themselves, to create and experience. Then I need to be able to assess their reactions so that I can indicate possibilities that they can explore further, in order to give them a sense of achievement and satisfaction.

PREPARATION OF WORK

Working in this way with living movement, it is very difficult to prepare work beforehand. Yet preparation is important in order to select the music and themes that it may be possible to use. Also, the composition of the group may be quite different from one session to another, certain patients having left or others joined, so that the unity of the group is different, or someone has a problem which is affecting the others.

How then does one start a session?

PREPARATION OF THE BODY FOR ACTION

1. *Preliminary preparation*

It is important on all occasions to "limber-up," to loosen up, in order to free the circulation and the joints, to prevent pulled muscles, to liven up the body and mind generally and to set the atmosphere.

To prepare the body for action, human beings and animals both instinctively stretch or wriggle. Waking in the morning, unwilling to get out of bed, we stretch and yawn and twist; a dog getting out of its basket also stretches and perhaps will roll and kick and get up and shake itself. A cat asleep in front of the fire may stretch a paw out even before it opens its eyes, then extend itself fully as though feeling the space around it while enjoying the warmth. So not only do we prepare the body for activity, we also awake to our surroundings. In changing from lying prone to standing up we get a different point of view. Anyone having pored over a book or a desk may shake his head and squeeze up his eyes to rid himself of the tensions of concentration, before getting out of his chair.

It is natural to make such preliminary preparation. Athletes make a point of exercising before going on the track, and while awaiting the signal for "off" will continue to make all kinds of small movements until the expected moment arrives.

Dancers start with what they call a "warm-up," but if that term is used, patients are likely to say: "I'm quite warm thank you" and continue to stand about.

Limbering-up also gives the leader time to sense all the things I have mentioned about the state of the group, and quite often one can pick up something that someone is doing and develop from that.

2. *Limbering-up*

There are various ways of limbering-up, but generally these may be classified as shaking, stretching, swinging, clapping, and rubbing.

Each of these ways can be utilised to develop any of the basic principles. Such limbering-up needs to be playful, to provoke fun and laughter and an easing of tension. If it is taken too seriously, it will only increase tension.

Shaking and stretching, particularly, give a patient an easy way to begin. He is not requested to use his whole body at first, and by concentrating on different parts in turn he can "feel" his way to extend his range, and if there is any physical disability or inhibition it is not so evident except to the leader, who then has more chance of adapting the work so that all can attempt it.

Patients can be asked to shake. Each part of the body can be shaken in turn, starting with hands, seeing they are quite relaxed from the wrists, shaking them up and down, from side to side, and round and round, going on to elbows, shoulders and head and chest.

Shoulders are often stiff, raising them towards the ears and letting them drop suddenly tests how much people can do. If they cannot manage this, it may be due to some traumatic condition. They may be weighed down with care, or are having to "shoulder" more responsibility than they can cope with. In the same way legs can be shaken, isolating foot, knee and hip, concentrating on what part is active and what part is passive. People can test if their knees are loose by raising the leg and letting it drop. The leg can be thrown out in different directions from the hip to ease its tensions.

Since the introduction of dances like the "Twist," people find it much easier to shake their seats than previously, and this movement now seems to be an important part of modern social dancing.

Shaking can be done with the whole body. When this is tried, attention should be paid to the head, which also should respond. Awareness is often slow to come in the shoulder-blades, the chest and diaphragm and the various areas of the back. Shaking can be done individually, or with a partner or a group.

It is always important to invent and change the way even a simple theme is presented, so that it does not become boring and automatic. A resistance has grown up against traditional P.T. amongst patients, probably because it has been presented in a monotonous, repetitive manner, and so has dulled interest and created a refusal to participate. It is so easy for sick people to fall back into inertia, and one's ingenuity is constantly taxed to stimulate activity and creativity.

(*a*) *Stretching.* Extending the body so that each muscle is fully stretched is as necessary as loosening-up in order to tone the muscles before an activity. In order to stretch there has first to be a folding in, and for each expansion a new direction should be explored, which should end taut from the finger-tips to the toes, with a gradual or quick release. This extension should be stressed with patients but not insisted on, for many insecure people find it impossible to open out even an arm or a fist, let alone the fingers, though to be able to risk it is an important step.

Adding the qualities of time and energy, the stretch could be varied in the employment of the specific elements and in increase and decrease.

(b) *Swinging.* Patients usually find it difficult to let the weight of the limb or trunk initiate the swing, for though it is a natural rhythm many people have never discovered their own rhythm. Because our bodies vary in weight, time should be allowed for people to find out that their weight affects the swing. Then they can adjust the speed to fit in with other people.

Patients also find balance difficult, so holding hands in a circle can help to steady them while they swing their legs, or they can hold hands with a partner.

So many people tend to swing as though they were a metronome, whereas a true swing is like a pendulum, in which there is an interplay between letting-go and control in waiting for the moment when weight changes the direction of the swing.

(c) *Slapping and rubbing.* On very cold days, slapping is a good way of stirring the circulation when people really do need to "warm-up," and this should always be done up the legs and arms towards the heart, and the same with rubbing.

Not only does this "warm" but it can liven up people who are very lethargic. Even the sound of slapping, if it has an accented phrasing, can be exhilarating. Again, force and time are in use.

Stamping and drumming on the floor with the feet and hands alternately, or beating with the hands on the floor and then shaking them in the air as high as possible are somewhat allied to slapping in their effect.

Rubbing is calmer than slapping, but can also exhilarate and warm.

(*d*) *Clapping.* Clapping hands all round the body, both dimensionally and diagonally, going on to clap hands with a partner, or moving around the room to the rhythm of the clapping and stopping to clap hands with other people can be another means of limbering-up.

Often it is unnecessary to be so detailed in the approach to limbering-up, a theme can be used which introduces several of these ways. For example, a group moving in a circle can shake one arm to the centre and then to the periphery, involving stretching which could change to a swing, using different body parts.

A rhythm can start with clapping or stamping, then be taken into different body parts, into locomotion and using variations of force or energy, time and space, changing to stretch or swing if required.

Limbering-up can be likened to the tuning of an orchestra, and is an introduction to "body awareness." We are concerned with "*what we move*," the different parts, the weight of the limbs, trunk and head are really felt as belonging. So many people concentrate movement in their limbs that the necessity for this awareness cannot be over-stressed.

In sickness, whether mental or physical, discomfort is noticeable both in posture and gesture. Physical pain shows in contraction, and adjustment so that the part that hurts is given the least amount to do, as in a limp. So, too, people who are depressed tend to be folded into themselves, and lack freedom of movement. But this is only a general indication and it is very important not to jump to conclusions about what one sees in a cursory way.

Some patients just shuffle or mooch along, concerned with what is occupying them inwardly. Others reverse this; by cutting off from their inner state, they then become able to move. Only when they try to function as a whole being do they find they are incapable of movement. Often a period when they do not attempt to do more movement than is demanded by normal living can enable them to come back, and then if one can find another approach they may benefit very much.

These Principles of Movement may appear to some people

21

very bald, too rigid, only physically practical. But as I see them, they serve a purpose. In studying art, a painter is trained in anatomy, he learns about the skeleton and how the muscles fit on, how the joints move, and so on. But when he comes to paint, say, a portrait, all that knowledge is so built into him that he does not need to think about it. Yet if he comes up against a difficulty he then may see that he has missed some of the structure which underlies the vitality and expressiveness of the face he is attempting to portray.

A musician, again, finding he cannot achieve the interpretation he is trying to express, goes back to simple basic technique, or he examines his instrument to see if it needs any attention; and he then can return to the work he is studying and often finds that he has the requisite command of his instrument, so that his whole attention can be given to his performance.

In a similar way, a patient is faced with a difficulty, whether it be physical or psychological. There are many ways of helping him to deal with the problem, and in movement, dance and drama he may find his release, or a help towards his healing.

CHAPTER III

Movement Themes and Sequences as Starting-points

WHEN, as frequently happens, it is not possible to work to a plan, it is of great assistance to have at the back of one's mind some simple themes which can be considered as starting-points, to be developed according to the immediate need of the situation.

DEVELOPING A THEME

For instance, take such a theme as "meeting and parting." It would be possible to begin with one of the basic principles, *e.g.* body awareness.

1. Different parts of the body meeting (*see* Fig. 7(*a*)), a hand could be taken to meet a knee, taken away again, then to a shoulder and a heel in succession, creating a movement sequence.

2. Two parts could move simultaneously towards each other—elbow to thigh, elbow to elbow (*see* Fig. 7(*b*)).

3. Such ideas could be played with and developed in the following ways:

    (*a*) Meeting and parting.
    (*b*) Meeting and passing.
    (*c*) Meeting and staying together to do something.
    (*d*) Meeting and clashing.

4. Add the principle of relationship. The four ways of working in 3(*a*)–(*d*) above could be carried on between partners, either using the idea of particular body parts, *e.g.* a hand meeting a

(*a*) Hand and foot   (*b*) Elbow and thigh

Fig. 7   Two body parts meeting

knee, two hips passing, backs clashing, or of a whole person, so that each is aware of the entirety of the other.

I have used this idea on a training course, where the members first moved about freely keeping to the order of 3(*a*)–(*d*) above as they met, and then having to observe each other as they approached so that both would react in a similar way.

One man training to be a nursing tutor said it had never before occurred to him how much one could tell about a person when merely passing by them.

5. From there, keeping the idea of partners, qualities of movement could be stressed. Each partner could be given a character involving certain motion factors or basic actions.

One could be a "presser" and the other a "floater," and the same theme of "meeting and parting" could be continued, the partners meeting and attempting to keep their own character and seeing if they influenced each other.

6.   Building from this, a space idea could be introduced, so that partners moving with certain qualities could move at varying levels, or could alternately relate to each other and then to the objects or room around them.

7.   A piece of music could be chosen and a dance set to it on the same meeting and parting theme.

On one occasion, I introduced such a dance to a group of schizophrenics and we needed an extra couple. One of the assisting group, who was talking to a patient who had hardly ever joined in anything beyond occasionally using her hands, suggested they might fill the gap and this woman immediately got up and went through the whole dance.

THE BUILD-UP

1. *New ideas*

Once the theme has been decided, it is then possible to build up or develop it by the addition of any one of the following ideas, some of which were shown in the example on pp. 23 and 24.

USE OF THE BODY	Exploring different parts
	Changes in locomotion: walking, running, leaping, jumping, turning
	Moving alone, with a partner or in a group formation
	Anchoring one part of the body and then moving the rest
	Balancing on different parts
	Leading with one part of the body, the rest following
	Moving with hands clasped behind back, or holding knees or ankles
STIMULUS	Rhythm, phrasing, accent, impulse, impact, regular beat and irregular rhythm, pause

25

MOVEMENT PRINCIPLES	Qualities of movement: energy, time, space, flow
	Increase and decrease in energy and time
	Gradations from exaggerated strength, almost cramp, to great delicacy, fine touch
	Gradations of sustainment and suddenness
	Gradations of directness and flexibility
	Gradations of flow, free or bound and controlled
	Space: levels, dimensions and diagonals
	Pathways, floor patterns
	Shape: round, flat, pointed
	Symmetric and asymmetric movement
	Simultaneous and successive movement
	Jumps, elevation
	Turns
MUSIC	Adding an accompaniment
	Fitting a theme to music
	Creating a dance
DRAMA	Imaginative idea
	Dramatic idea
	Mime
DIMENSIONS	Closing and opening
	Growing and shrinking
	Narrow and wide
	Near and far
	Drawing letters or shapes, either as floor pattern or gesture
SPACE	Personal and general space
	Establishing one's own place, going away from and returning to it
	Deciding on certain points in the room, moving between them, keeping the focus on each point in turn
OPPOSITES	Question and answer
	Action and response
	Attack and defence

PARTNER AND   Working with a partner
GROUP WORK   Group sensitivity
Wings, *i.e.* one person in the centre of a line of people directs them as though they were his wings, either holding hands or conducting

Ideas can be evoked by a picture or an advertisement, in fact, anything observed can stimulate imagination. Ruth St. Denis invented a dance from a cigarette poster she had noticed.

2. *Word association*

A theme could be set by stringing verbs together:
Swinging, lifting, dropping, rising, running, stopping.
Waving, shooting forward, pausing, turning, pouncing.
Reaching up high, spiralling down, closing in and exploding.

Such sequences can be built on either in movement or in a dramatic way.

Another way of using words is to take one word and see what other words can be associated with it; this can stimulate imagination and invention, and lead to a very creative work.

Take such a word as ROUND. What could it suggest?

Circle	ball	moon	planet
barrel	tub	circus	plate

To develop from the word CIRCLE, we could think of it as enclosing space or dividing space, or as having an imaginary central point as the focus of the movement. Immediately we are bringing in shape.

The circle can move backwards and forwards, sideways, up and down, when the stress is on space.

What movement of the body could develop from here, and would it be possible to add varying qualities such as swinging, crouching, creeping, stamping, and so on? The movement idea could be reduced to something very simple. Imagine a group of psychiatric patients, long-term geriatrics. They often like to hold hands in a circle, they then feel contained and safe, and they can communicate through touch. Swaying, bending, stretching, using knees can all be done without

27

letting go, and they may even get brave enough to put a foot towards the centre, or take a step, or drop hands and turn round, and then the circle can move as a whole, towards and away from the centre and round and round, gradually building in other ideas.

One person or more could go into the centre and treat the circle as a wall that they try and get through, the circle can try and prevent them or let them through.

The circle can be broken and form a single line, and then divide again, and each line can go off on its own and meet the others; then groups may form.

The idea of PLAYING BALL hardly needs enlarging on. Patients often enjoy miming a game, throwing and catching, kicking, dribbling, balancing a ball on different parts of the body. The size and shape of balls can be played with, the ball could turn into a globe or a moon.

On one training course, I gave the theme ROUND; the students worked in four groups.

One made a circle round a clown who was twirling a plate in mime on his finger, while the group moved around him, and it developed into a little dance drama.

The second created a dance based entirely on circular movement and shape.

The third took the idea of a "barrel," and enacted a scene in an inn, stocking up and serving and drinking.

The fourth started with a tub, feeding pigs, which led to a whole farmyard scene, buckets and a well all arising from the original idea.

At one hospital, a group was given the theme of "rolling barrels," which they mimed, several together rolling their barrels the length of the room. On arrival, they were asked what they should do with them, and in each case the barrel was up-ended and opened and they were all drinking, and telling us what drink each had chosen.

Another use of word association is to gather ideas from the group; sometimes it will be one idea, but it may be that each one will give a word, and these can be woven together to make a story.

By a group of children I was once given: a fairy—a knight— a policeman—cats and kittens—a horse—outer space.

The boy who chose to be "outer space" tired of whirling around on his own and became a "kiwi" on another planet. Between us, we made up the following story.

The knight was looking through his telescope and spotted some disturbance going on in the sky; he thought he should investigate, so he called for his horse, only to find it had gone lame, so he took it to the fairy, who cured it. Then the knight enlisted the help of the policeman; while they were making preparations to go to the planet, the kiwi was being attacked by the cats and kittens from yet another planet, and as they greatly outnumbered him he was having much difficulty in preventing them landing. However, just in time the knight and the policeman were shot off in a rocket and were able to subdue the invaders.

I realise that tabulated in this way, these suggestions appear bald and dry, but I find in a given situation, to be able quickly to think up an idea starts the ball rolling, and the imagination not only of the leader but of the whole group can be stimulated and something creative produced, however slight.

CHAPTER IV

Specific Ways of Using Movement in Therapy

In the following pages, an attempt will be made to indicate how these movement principles can be utilised in treatment, based on experience with patients, sometimes with individuals who were at the same time undergoing depth analysis or psychotherapy, sometimes with a group.

Working with one patient alone, it is possible for activities to be more detailed and directly related to personal problems. These problems, though unique in the context of the patient's own conditioning, temperament and experience, have certain underlying similarities, for instance, the experience of rejection by the father or mother.

Naturally, this rejection may happen in different ways; the mother or father may die, or the parents be divorced, the child may suffer from a stepmother or stepfather, or feel ousted by a brother or sister. Either parent may suffer from accident or illness, or may have a violent disposition or may be under the domination of a partner. The mother may fail in giving the child enough care, attention, handling or affection, or father may be indifferent, aggressive, and fail to play his part in introducing the child to the world. These and corresponding problems are constantly being met with, but each rejection is individual and presents particular difficulties to the person concerned.

Therefore at every session it is vital to work from what the patient contributes, according to the state he or she may be in at any given moment.

So what should be our approach?

Professor Tibble in summing up a discussion on the difference between teaching and therapy at a working party on music for

30

the handicapped at Leamington Spa, said it seemed to him that in teaching, if one came to a block, one could work directly on trying to move or overcome it, but in therapy it could not be dealt with in this way. It had to be gone around, and conditions created whereby it could be dissolved. In other words, in education a direct approach to a difficulty can be used, whereas in therapy an indirect approach is needed. It goes without saying, however, that the two approaches overlap and inter-relate, for coping with a failure in education may need a "going around" approach and re-education by direct methods comes into therapy.

During a course of treatment, a patient may go through many phases, and though these phases may be common to many, they will not follow the same pattern or order in experience or content.

Hence I stress again the need for observation, because it is necessary to be with the person in feeling and thought in order to establish relationship, trust and confidence.

PLAY—ITS IMPORTANCE IN PERSONAL DEVELOPMENT

Besides particular traumatic experiences, many people seem to have missed out on "play" in their childhood, because of home or other circumstances. Mother has had no time to spend with the child apart from caring for his immediate needs, so that there has been no stimulation of curiosity, inventiveness, imagination or discovery. Father is mostly at work and seldom sees him. For safety or convenience, the baby may have been kept in a pram, baby-bouncer, run-about, or playpen for such lengths of time that his activity has been curtailed, either by preventing him from crawling, so not using and developing his arms and shoulders, or depriving him of using his legs in a variety of ways. Of course, it is very necessary to keep the baby within bounds, but I wonder very much whether the need of the child to explore is sufficiently realised by parents. In play, he can find his individual limits, boundaries and skills, especially if there is someone near whom he can trust; he can learn that some objects are to be avoided because they are dangerous, like electric power points, while others can amuse and entertain him.

The baby, to start with, seems to have no knowledge of his body (*see* reference to Preyer and Bernfeld in *The Image and Appearance of the Human Body*, by Paul Schilder, M.D., Ph.D., Routledge & Kegan Paul, 1925, p. 194), but from the time he is born, by twisting, turning and kicking, he becomes aware of it. From sucking the breast or bottle he goes on to suck a fist or foot or anything else within reach, including objects such as a spoon, rattle or cuddly toy. This is the beginning of play. He finds he can yell and coo, he can hold a hand tightly, he can blow bubbles, he can roll his head slowly, or shake it quickly, he can hit out, or curl and twist his legs, using all the kinaesthetic and motor qualities. "We do not know very much about our body unless we move it. Movement is a great uniting factor between the different parts of our own body" (Schilder, *op. cit.*, p. 112).

In all these ways, the baby builds some sense of his own identity. Gradually he gets the idea *he* can touch *his* toes, *he* wants to roll over, and *he* finds what *he* can do. F. Reitman, writing in *Psychotic Art* (Routledge and Kegan Paul, 1950, p. 54), refers to the individual's feeling of "Me, here, now." *See* also pages 53–4 in his book.

With this growing awareness of the body, there seems to be also the growth of what could be described as "body-image," that is, how his body appears to the baby himself, and through sensation and perception he develops sensitivity and command over his body: "I want to do this; I see how I can do it. I do it." This leads on to play. "The image of the human body means the picture of our own body, which we form in our mind, that is the way in which we appear to ourselves (Schilder, *op. cit.*, p. 11).

Peter Slade in *Experience of Spontaneity* (Longmans, 1968, p. 30), refers to play as personal and projected: "Although all play is fluid, the only genuine division . . . is between personal and projected. Projected play is when the individual is generally quiet in his body, and projects out of his mind a dream or idea into, on to or around objects outside himself. Then the objects take on life. Personal play is where the individual gets up and does the thing himself." In personal play, seeing himself in the roles he has invented, a child extends his knowledge of himself and his own boundaries, and in projecting his inner world into the outer world through play, he can become aware of his relationship to things and learn to adapt to changing situations both pleasant and unpleasant.

In both forms, the child plays out his imagination and fantasy, and has the opportunity to act out feelings and disturbances, called by Peter Slade "the spitting-out process." I remember during the war a little girl saying to me: "We never used to play war games before the war, now all our games are fighting."

The child can also experience the joy of creation, of forming something for himself, of being involved both inwardly and outwardly and he develops his capacity for absorption and concentration.

Such play involves movement and drama and is the stage following the baby's first explorations. Thus early in life comes this interaction between body and body-image, the inner and the outer, through which psychic attitudes are built up. "This building is a process of investing objects outside oneself with significance (so leading to symbols, 3Rs, etc. in learning and learning about organisation). In personal play we invest ourselves with significance and here it is important to have a reasonably correct body and drama image." (Slade, *op. cit.*, p. 1.)

The body is the instrument we use in the give and take of life; through it, we communicate in speech and action, and receive impressions and reactions.

The baby who has jumped up and down on his parents' laps, has clambered all over them, has been picked up, carried, swung around, and has embraced them and been cuddled and has learned to walk and run with them, whose parents have entered into his play with objects, bats, balls, bricks, etc. develops relationship and communication, and learns to express himself, and take the knocks of life; his whole body has become a part of him.

LACK OF PLAY IN CHILDHOOD

I have known patients with little or no awareness in their bodies, and have found that there had been no opportunity for play in their childhood. They recoil from physical contact, yet when touched they cannot tell which part of them is being touched, though they may feel the warmth of a hand. They may be able to move a part, yet not be aware of that part moving unless they can feel it in relation to someone's hand. Yet they can look after themselves, hold down a job and drive a car, and their bodies function normally. But they only see this happening: hands picking up a kettle, feet walking—there is practically no sensation. I have queried whether there could be some neurological cause, but there has been no evidence of such, and subsequent development has confirmed this.

No one, however, can return to the unselfconsciousness of the child, and imagination, creativity, absorption, and ability to relate may remain latent, undeveloped and unrealised. Even if an adult builds sand-castles with children, plays with toys and trains, he cannot re-enter that state of childhood.

How, then, can we come to know and release these potentialities if they have not already started to develop?

Unfortunately, in many cases, people have become so set in their attitudes that they are afraid of attempting anything, they feel too self-conscious and do not want to display their incompetence, or express themselves. In fact, of course, we all reveal ourselves continually in our movement or lack of it, in our speech and our silence.

HOW PLAY AND MAKE-BELIEVE CAN BE EXPLORED AND EXPERIENCED BY ADULTS

In movement, dance and drama we have a medium through which absorption can be experienced, playfulness indulged, fantasy given rein without becoming too diffuse, and emotions played out without any loss of face! Here the child in us can find a place where it can breathe, grow and find itself, where we can relate to this child in ourselves, and lead it gently by the hand to join up with our maturer selves. Often a work of art is created, and if it is only appreciated by the players and perhaps one observer, it gives a lasting satisfaction and fulfilment.

When this happens, qualities unknown come to light, some we like, some we may not like; but they are all part of us, and if we can learn to live with both sides of our natures, and use the drives, imagination and the latent qualities we did not know we possessed, these will contribute to our wholeness (*see* Goldstein in Schilder, *op. cit.*, pp. 207–8).

Rudolf Laban would sometimes take a class where the students were asked to imagine they were newly-born, and to experiment for themselves to find out how movement develops. Even the conventional student found the experience both fascinating and exhilarating.

Some patients can work in this way, and for those who have never known what it is to play, a new dimension may

Fig. 8 Crawling

open up, especially for those who are not at ease in their bodies. Once when talking to a patient about the baby's first movement I happened to say I could no longer put a big toe to my mouth, whereupon she tried to do so herself, and by degrees learned to play with her limbs. She discovered that when pressing one foot on the other it was not like pressing on the floor, it was spongy and flexible, and she became aware of the fan-shaped bones in her feet. When crawling (*see* Fig. 8) she felt her back as a bridge between her hands and her feet and slowly a sense of personal identity began to dawn and a relationship with space and objects around, revealing a world of adventure and play.

Once I was asked to work with a group on "body-image." After each patient had traced the shape of one of his hands with the other and felt the outline and shape of his body, I unrolled a length of paper and each pencilled outlines of their hands and feet. One schizophrenic with whom we could make no verbal contact beyond a greeting and who was able to follow little of what we did, having put his own hand and foot in their imprints, tried to do the same with his opposite number's hand print, and evidently realised it was different from his own, for he moved round until he could put his own hand so that it fitted the imprint, which meant an entire adjustment of his body.

A patient who has suffered rejection may be crying out inside for "Mum" or may have shut himself away from all feeling, so that the outside world cannot affect him. Often we see people moving about with their arms folded in front of them, and in addition they may have sunken chests and heads, which might signify "I'm holding on to the little I've got," or "I've been so hurt I can only hold on to myself," or "I'm defending myself against all-comers." Or, indeed, other things. The body is then closed in.

SPACE—USED AS A PROGRESSION TOWARDS GREATER AWARENESS

As an instance of the patient whose attitude is "I want my Mum," wide, reaching-out movements either horizontally or vertically may be indicative of what they are feeling, though this may be first attempts to reach consciousness or just to find any expression at all. Again, I would stress the importance of accurate observation, as there may be other movement factors that alter the meaning.

Patients may be unable to work in a group, or if in a group, keep themselves apart, using their own movement and ideas and ignoring whatever else is going on. The individual can be left to follow or disregard as he wills any direction given to the group as a whole, and some can carry on their own exploration and may be drawn in by degrees to work with the rest. Others need to be worked with individually.

Such physical expression of the desire for the unattainable

may need to continue for some considerable time before any other theme is suggested.

To explore the space around the body from "reaching-out" through the whole range from fully extended to quite close to the body, all the time experimenting in turn with relation to the outer world, and relation to oneself, within the immediate space around the body, is the experience of general and personal space. "Experience in pathology . . . leads me to the conclusion that the psychological space concerning one's own body is different from other space . . . The outside space and the body space differ in their structure" (Schilder, *op. cit.*, p. 57). Exploring such psychological space is also part of developing a visual image of one's own being.

Changing from "I want my Mum," which reaches virtually to infinity, to working close to the body can give the feeling of "being a person," protected, safe, but it can also bring the realisation "I have no Mum," with all the attendant distress. Then we may get the complete opposite, that of closing in, either in defence, or to contain the hurt. We must then be very careful not to force that person to open out even if it means they stay closed in and inhibited. It is sometimes possible, especially for those spoken of earlier who habitually go around clasping themselves, to suggest opening out a hand, that is, when working close to the body to go out towards the world. But often people cannot manage even such a small movement; perhaps they could then be asked to make some space between their arms and their bodies, still with folded arms. Sometimes people come to a standstill and are unable to pursue movement for a time, and this can happen to someone with a normally good movement vocabulary.

When it is realised that sad, hurtful experiences often come into consciousness gradually, and indeed need to be so experienced to prevent an overwhelming uprush of affect, then such inhibition is understandable. If patients can still move, their movement may be repetitive, confined as to space, or simply swaying or rocking, and as the painful past comes to light a backward movement may become impossible.

The person who has come to such an impasse in movement may be coming to a dawning awareness of the emotions that the child in his helplessness was forced to repress, against those who had caused him to suffer, and any movement is resisted, especially with other people. We then have to use invention and imagination and utilise anything that occurs to us or may be to hand. Perhaps a patient can produce a painting or model, which might suggest a further step in movement, and it may be that more than one approach is needed at any one session.

USE OF OBJECTS TO EMPHASISE EXTERNAL REALITY

I have arranged furniture to depict certain points in a patient's painting; for instance, three strokes joined at the base I represented by two armchairs facing each other with the seats touching. I then asked the patient to see if they could be separated. By moving the chairs apart, the strokes, which had given a vague idea of father, mother and child, were again drawn in a quick sketch, this time in distinct recognisable pin figures, separated and having changed position. With each arrangement of the furniture suggested by the previous sketch a new idea was invoked, leading to some insight.

Working with sketches was also used in alternation with hitting a punchball, and a movement suggestion. In each case there was some little development during the session, but much repetition was needed and the same problems came up over and over again, though each sequence of sketches showed some progression, however much the insight was lost in the intervening days.

Wherever one is working, there are sure to be objects one can use and play with. Every hall has at least walls, a ceiling, floor and doors, and probably some furniture; so, too, has a room. Once I asked a patient to explore the room (*see* Fig. 9), and she suddenly realised that this was something she had never done, for as a child she was shut in a room while her mother was at work in another part of the building, and she never dared to move. The experience of finding out her surroundings, and that there was a door through which she could pass, was a revelation.

In a games room or gymnasium there could be tennis-balls, table-tennis bats and balls, medicine balls, a punchball and all kinds of apparatus. Such objects can not only be played with

Fig. 9   Feeling an object: exploring

or used for gymnastics, they can play a part in bringing a sense of reality of the outer world, and may also draw off excess emotion—if only to give an opportunity for letting off steam.

In a psychiatric hospital in Holland I have watched a movement therapist playing basket-ball with male patients of varying ability, from really tough, athletic youths to older men, slow in both mind and body. It was really exciting to see his skill in using and directing the ball, so that he called out the maximum from every patient without taxing his ability beyond what he could manage. It was a lesson in how to adapt and apply a skill to the needs of patients.

The many kinds of odd ploys or hobbies I have at various times attempted, without any thought of their being useful, have come in handy, as well as special studies I have undertaken.

COMING TO TERMS WITH AGGRESSION

1. *Dealing with violence*

In life generally we all have our share of aggressive emotions and instincts, and need to come to terms with them as far as we can.

The problem of dealing with violence in people undergoing treatment is a constant challenge, even though with present-day drugs it is possible to ease the condition. Very often the inner ferment is such that the patient dare not give expression to it for fear of being swamped and engulfed, or it may break out in wild storms of rage, anger, fury or desperation.

Those who have suffered repression, trauma, who have insufficiently developed egos, or who have found no channel into which to direct their energies, have an infinitely greater task in meeting the external threats of life and those destructive powers over which we have no control, against which we have little protection.

Yet these fears may be so deep-seated that, as one person put it to me: "I only want to beat my father, but that doesn't get me anywhere, it is only a cover for the fear which is too deep for me to reach."

Some do not understand as much as that, and are just consumed by the explosive feelings and the desire to hit out. They become identified with destructive forces, and so caught that they live them out in all kinds of violent acts instead of learning to live with them.

As well as being given drugs, people with the aid of depth analysis or psychotherapy can work to integrate their positive and negative attitudes. In addition, creative activities provide means for obtaining greater insight and can act also as an outlet. Pottery, modelling, drawing and painting can be used for expressing these inner states.

Patients find digging, breaking clay, bouncing balls against a wall, smashing already broken china, and so on, are forms of expressing violence in a way which does not harm other people. A punchball has value in that it can respond without having its own affect and some people need to experience their anger against something that is resistant, but may not be able to express it to another person, or they may be so uncontrolled that to evoke that anger may be dangerous. The punchball can take a lot of punishment and people discover different ways of using it. If they are not very certain about taking its response they can slap it with an open hand from side to side, as though boxing someone's ears, and having got used to that, then use a fist to punch it directly in front of them. If very frightened they need only to touch it and feel it give, or they can smooth their hands over it, feeling its sensitivity to a light touch.

Someone when very angry can have a real "punch-up" and may at the end find out what has caused their anger, which was not clear before. Or they can beat it instead of beating themselves. They can beat it up with all the venom at their disposal, imagining it as the object of their hatred, working afterwards on their relationship with the person concerned in their analytical sessions.

A punchball is of particular importance because, being attached, the aggression can be focused. However, if no punchball is available, cushions can be used as a substitute, but then the aggression has not the same boundaries—the cushion can be flung anywhere (*see* Fig. 10). On two occasions in my experience when cushions were being used, aggression did nearly get out of hand. Once it was directed at me, but at the last minute the patient controlled it. On the second occasion, the woman involved had been so afraid of killing if her fury were aroused that she had never dared to "let go," therefore when I piled a heap of cushions and invited her to attack them, imagining they were her mother, her intention to kill was more violently activated than I had anticipated and she was savage in her action. Yet some while later she told me that at the very moment of release of her desire to kill, she, for the first time, realised that the act of killing was not inevitable, but that she had the power of choice.

Besides those whose movement-capacity changes, there are those who are constantly limp and inert, and those who are so tense that they are more or less in a state of cramp, yet if they have an emotional outburst become remarkably strong; it appears that the strength is latent and takes possession of

Fig. 10 The cushion can be flung anywhere

and uses them. In both cases, they have no command over their strength and cannot employ it voluntarily.

This inability to experience or use strength which is latent is a problem to many patients.

A girl whose natural movement was sustained and flowing and whose strength was only seen in her unconscious movement, complained of feeling empty and non-existent, yet at the same time overwhelmed with violent impulses she couldn't express. When I began to work towards strength with this girl she found her expression of it was so exaggerated that she was in a state of cramp. Once when moving to exciting music this cramp was released, and she felt as if threatened by external forces.

This girl, having experienced the cramp physically, related it to holding on to her feelings and when she let go she was overcome by this fear from the outside threat. The result of all this she discussed with her analyst as we went along and became able to use strength at will in a functional way, with no fear or threat, nor of inability to control or not.

One young man, wanting desperately to relate to, and live, a normal life, was unable to use his strength. He always wanted to approach movement through drama, but when

Fig. 11   Pitting one's strength against another

really pinned down and driven to pit his strength against the leader (*see* Fig. 11) and then against a wall, managed to find there was that side to him, and the opposition and resistance had evoked it; but he could not initiate it by himself. However, he had appreciated this treatment, had appreciated being given bounds and limits, and complained of too much permissiveness in the attitude of some members of staff. He began to realise that in drama one has to use movement principles and that strength was part of these principles.

Another woman patient wrote: "At one time I had a great deal of aggression, this movement to music was one very good way of using up the aggression. I felt I could do this even with other people close to me, whilst ordinarily at this time I feel afraid of being near people because of my aggression."

2. *The leader's role in containing emotive material*

When such release is experienced, it is important to have the therapist present. He may not need to be active, but the fact that he is observing, understanding and "experiencing with" the patient can give a certain security. He is also alert to act if necessary or suggest changes in the movement to redirect the explosive energies, which the patient is afraid will become uncontrollable when by himself. Then such strength can be used constructively, by which I mean using the bodily experience, to quote Jung, as "an indirect way of approach to instinctual images" (C. G. Jung, *Modern Man in Search of a Soul*, Routledge and Kegan Paul, 1933, p. 46).

A teacher in a school for maladjusted children once told me that if she could have a child in a temper tantrum alone with her in a room, and really let him experience the full extent of his aggressive instincts, she never had the same trouble again, but that once when she was absent, one boy from her group was shut in alone and broke seventeen windows.

Adult patients have tried to use a piece of music which they had found stimulating in the group, but when alone they could not move to it. Others have tried to run a small group without help and again found the same result. The need seems to be to have someone present to preserve the bounds. I call it "holding the ring" until people can find their own "ring." With adults or big teenagers a lot of ingenuity is needed, as they cannot be held like a child, but the actual movement can act as a container when directed rightly.

3. *The place of body awareness in channelling instinctive drives and emotions*

When I was teaching in the school mentioned above there was one big boy who was a real menace. He was a great, hefty chap, but fat and flaccid. He used to beat up all and sundry. In order to try and get him to use his strength and not attack others, I once asked him to use his knees with a thrusting movement. Not only could he not attempt this, but on con-

44

sidering it afterwards it seemed to me that he ceased coming
to movement from that time, because in asking him to use his
knees I was trying to get him to have command over his
strength; his only idea of defence was to hit out with his fists,
and the only way of protecting himself was this enormous
show of aggression. My request must have seemed a terrifying
threat to him, depriving him of what he felt was his strength.

The idea of using knees in this way came from Rudolf Laban,
who once told me that, when working with disturbed people,
he had found getting them to use their knees could alter a
situation that was becoming ominous. Had I had more
experience I would probably have gone much more gradually.

As it was, days later, I was playing the piano in the hall
when this boy came up to me and asked if I knew a song
called "Lullaby." I said I knew several and asked if he could
sing one. To my amazement, he sang the Brahms' "Lullaby." On
my suggestion, he came to sing with me and also played the
piano. Only then did I see quite a different side to him. If
he made any mistake he became very agitated and went
compulsively back to the beginning and started again, as
though he couldn't bear to be wrong. When singing his
breathing was quite unrelated to the words, though he stoutly
maintained he was breathing correctly, until one day he said:
"Take too many breaths, don't I, Miss?" It seemed to me at
these times he was just a frightened baby, so no wonder he
was such a bully.

We talk of "kicking someone in the pants" and "elbowing
people out of our way." So elbows seem to have some con-
nection with the expression of irritation or anger, and I have
suggested to people having trouble with aggressive tendencies
that they might use their elbows to thrust all round them in
every direction, using a maximum amount of energy, not
necessarily directed at anything, but to get the feeling of
strength in the body, and they have found it a help in gaining
command of their feelings.

Patients, in fact people generally, are often very unaware of
these joints, especially the elbows, and they tend to use their
arms and legs as though they lacked any hinges, and could
only be used in one piece.

If patients cannot use strength, we need to find an acceptable way in which they can work towards experiencing it for themselves. We have to decide whether to give them a theme which, by the very suddenness of the demand, could bring a recognition that strength need not necessarily be destructive.

Quite often a punching movement can be asked for straight away, not primarily towards an object, but in order to obtain the bodily sensation required. I used this idea on one occasion and one woman who had been hitting out all over the place, in an amazed tone of voice said: "I could never have believed Audrey could get me to do that."

Sometimes there is the need to let people experiment from what they are able to do, extending their range by gradual degrees till they find they can manage what had seemed impossible. When patients who have displayed resistance to using their bodies discover they can make the effort and gain some command, it often brings a sense of achievement and freedom.

FANTASY UNRELATED TO LIFE

Some people, having retreated into a world of fantasy, invest everything with something from their own inner world; they feel themselves a vacuum and therefore can take no stock of their own identity in relation to objects or people. Their only sense of identity is in feeling the outside world as part of themselves. Consequently, great care is needed in handling them, for disintegration can be caused in trying to separate in order to relate.

Such people may continue to function in their ordinary lives, and also may be very creative and imaginative and intelligent, though they may see and depict the world as two-dimensional. When the fantasy and the sense of nothingness is very strong, the materials they use in these activities, instead of being the means to project themselves into their art, become an extension of themselves, so that they cannot attempt to stand back and view the contents objectively and in relationship to the world outside them.

Fantasy may go so far that a patient may deny that he has a body, or will insist that his body is unable to function, though in fact it is doing so quite normally. Some dissociate

46

in order to carry on their work, keeping their inner and outer selves apart. They can be very successful in what they do, though at times, when there is too much inner pressure, they may not be aware of the action of their bodies, and may not be able to attend to what is said to them to the point of not hearing at all.

It is difficult to find a contact if there is no desire on the patient's part to make some relatedness, but many really do want to become aware of, and to live more freely in, the world around them.

1. *Compulsive fantasy*

One woman came to me saying she was caught in a fantasy pattern; an S inside a circle in which she was confined (*see*

Fig. 12   Leading with an elbow, describing a figure-of-eight

Fig. 13), not being able to get out and no one being able to get in, and the whole time she was being swung around in it.

She also had dreamed of an ogress mother with an enormous head, and a huge swollen right foot and no body. In the dream the daughter, however, was not crushed but was dancing.

Fig. 13   The fantasy pattern

Amongst other things I worked with her on exploring the zones of space into which her limbs could move. Then leading with an elbow or a shoulder (*see* Fig. 12) and letting her body follow, she moved all over the room. In doing so, she was describing figures of eight. After some while I drew her attention to this pattern, and that one could look at it as two Ss joined at the centre, with no circle to contain them as in her fantasy.

48

The following week she came with a sketch (*see* **Fig. 13**). A horizontal figure of eight, one loop outlined in purple, the other in green, and below was the fantasy pattern, with a woman's head and only legs and feet, but where the top of the **S** touched the circle was a slight break. I pointed out that had the pattern been made with a piece of string, one could have taken it and whipped the whole pattern into a straight line. Later she brought me a model of a woman in a figure of eight, and with this the pattern and fantasy seemed to have dissolved. She only came a few more times, but always maintained that she had been enormously helped.

2. *Fantasy played out in a dramatic way or with objects*

These people, who live their fantasy, feel a security and a certain safety in the fantasy, so it is important not to ignore it, but to work towards objective reality.

Sometimes it is possible to use fantasy as a starting-point. A scene can be enacted using the patient's idea and seeing if it can be developed in some way that can help. Then, both the patient and the therapist enter into the action, but whereas to the patient it is probably pure fantasy, it behoves the therapist to be aware not only of the story as the patient sees and feels it, and as it unfolds, but at the same time to remain very conscious of the actual surroundings. For example, the story may be of walking over grass and round a tree, but the grass is the floor and the tree a chair. The aim should be to lead the scene gradually so that the objects, besides being part of the play, are also recognised for the material things they really are, and so that the realisation grows that they are being used in the "make-believe."

Here we have "objects" again, but this time the emphasis is on the fantasy, and how that can be utilised by introducing various ways of working. It may be that an object becomes so involved in the fantasy that it comes to mean something completely other than what it really is. Then to be touched or handled as the thing it is may cause dislike, because it no longer holds the subjective content. However, this is a step towards distinguishing the actual and the imagined, the outer and the inner, and can be an achievement and lead to other things being seen and held as external and separate, and put to their normal uses without dissociation. Then acceptance of the outside world becomes more possible.

An object can be played with by the patient and then shared with the therapist. When this happens, there may come a moment when in fantasy the patient has built a defence round himself, and the object can then be used to show what that defence stimulates in another person. It can be thrown to break through or jump over the defence, or simply put down to indicate the separation the defence has created, and the inability to effect a meeting.

In such play, it is essential to gauge how much the patient can stand; if an object is thrown too hard, or makes too much noise, it may only increase the fear or other emotion that has caused the defences to be put up in the first place. On the other hand, if judged accurately, it may make an impact, bringing some insight by the way it is presented and received.

Sometimes if one presses a patient too hard he may begin to feel he is disintegrating. Then picking up something that has become real to him at some time can help regain stability, or a fantasy may be evoked which indicated the former situation; if it can be linked to what has become real, and he be led to use it, he can rescue himself. I will give an instance of what I mean. A patient may feel he, or just a part of him, is being transported in some vessel which is in danger of foundering. Then, if he can play out doing the necessary repairs, salvaging the oars, catching hold of the quay with a boathook, or just baling out a boat, he gets the sensation that he can come to his own aid, and builds up a picture of himself as the rescuer. This mental picture can then be called up and used on further threatening occasions to create a sense of stability and safety and so prevent dissociation.

THE RELATIONSHIP OF BODY-IMAGE, BODY AWARENESS, FANTASY AND IMAGINATION

In order to use fantasy and imagination in these ways, the body has to be used, but many people are ill at ease in their bodies. They probably have no sense of "body-image," or they may appear to themselves quite other than they are, they may think parts of their bodies are out of shape when they are quite normal. They may dislike their own appearance, or may be disgusted by the natural functions, they may feel stiff, tense, awkward or ungainly, or they may feel themselves threatened by any physical contact, even of anything inanimate, and recoil from touching anything themselves, as well as from being touched.

Sometimes, when the dissociation is not so much to do with touch but has to do with surroundings, people and things are not normally discerned. Then one has to watch out for anything that might get hurt or broken—I once just prevented a T.V. set from being sent flying quite unintentionally.

It might be that working on "body awareness" could help some people; others, so unaware that they cannot tell where they are being touched, or who deny the actuality of their bodies, may not be able to start in this way—the fantasy life is too strong. Any direct concentration on their own bodies may be impossible, they may be incapable of making a deliberate, conscious movement of finger or hand, or even of watching a finger pointing.

THE PIANO USED TO DEVELOP RELATIONSHIP TO THE
OUTER WORLD

In such cases, a piano may be found useful. The response is entirely the result of the action of the player, and yet it has a voice of its own.

Basing what is done on piano technique, one can choose how best to approach an individual. Whether someone has studied the piano previously or not, I would start with primary work, either using the lid shut over the keys, or straight away on the keyboard.

The lid can convey the sensation of something immovable, known and safe, as a support, if only for the hand and arm, so producing a sense of trusting oneself to something else, something that can be touched without having to risk it hitting back.

It can be used to relax on to or away from, by resting the finger-tips, then dropping the wrist loosely. The arm can then be pulled away to test the relaxation, when the whole hand and arm should drop.

All kinds of touching can be tried out, gripping tightly with the finger-tips, putting them down stiffly, firmly, lightly, slowly, suddenly, with a bang, smoothing, caressing or tapping.

When the keyboard is used, the principle is the same but listening enables one to discriminate as to whether the keys have been depressed in a way that will produce the sound required. The pianistic aim is to use the weight of the arm to depress the keys, and the finger-tips for agility. Incidentally, piano-playing is also helped!

In order to gain such control the following exercises are invaluable, not only for piano practice, but in many other ways.

1. With the finger-tips touching the ivories of the keys, knuckles slightly raised, the wrist easy and in line with the arm. Let the weight of the arm depress the keys together.

2. Keeping the keys depressed in this way, each finger in turn can be lifted and slowly put down in a single smooth movement right through to the keybed, without a jerk.

Naturally there can be various developments from these exercises, the sequence of the fingers can be changed, major, minor and diminished triads can be used, and the same technique applied when starting to learn a new piece.

Using hands to make an instrument speak, listening to the sound, to the quality, to rhythm, is learning to "pay attention" to something other than oneself. A dialogue can then be held between the player and the piano, and it gradually is taken for the separate entity it is, where before it may have been caught up in the fantasy. The different voices that can speak back according to the way the keys are played show the result of different actions, and are an indication of how we both cause reactions and react ourselves in our personal relationships.

The actual physical control also can bring a sense of the reality of hands, and what they can do; how relaxation and strength can combine with time, developing patience, absorption, concentration and perseverance by working in such a minimal way, but rewarding when hands can really transfer ideas and wishes into sound with great variety of speed and quality. Then the piano from being just an object becomes a true musical instrument.

The inner mechanism of the piano can also be pointed out, and people find it interesting to see how what they do on the keyboard sets this mechanism in motion. This again stresses the recognition of the outside world or object.

I have had an intelligent three-year-old boy change from a really disturbed state to complete absorption for half-an-hour at a time by playing a note, listening to the sound, meanwhile watching the action of the hammers, and using the pedals. He always indicated the exact moment when the sound ceased.

Because the piano was my own main instrument it was the obvious choice for me, but any instrument can be used.

USE OF MUSIC

1. *Examples of therapy*

On one occasion three patients using a piano, an Indian pipe and a maraca, and myself with an Eastern gong, improvised, then set and recorded what we had invented. One of them, who up till then had been restricted and repetitive in her movement, suddenly took the floor and began dancing all over the room in a far freer way than I had ever seen her use before; then another patient came in and listened, and afterwards said: "That's exactly what they do. I've been in India."

I have also found that music coupled with movement has been a means of establishing communication with an autistic child. She was a girl of about six, and was the first autistic child I had taken alone. She was also diagnosed as a near-catatonic. She came ten times, each of ten minutes' duration, over a period of five months.

The first time when I fetched her she got up and came without demur when I took her hand, and let me sit her down and remove her shoes, but she was like a puppet, with no volition of her own. I got no response when I tried to get her to jump, or go down to the floor, or play with hands, though she would walk round the room with me. I sang all the time, anything that came into my head, making up tunes and rhythms as well.

Having not got anywhere with her in this way, I took her arms and gently opened them a little way and closed them again. She smiled as I let them return but seemed a bit scared when I took them apart, and in the end resisted, so I stopped at once.

Then I went to the piano and played, and this caught her attention. So, as I played, I tapped the rhythm on her hand with one hand, and then took her hand and tapped the rhythm with it, still playing with my other hand. The next time I was at the piano she took my free hand and bumped it on the piano, trying to pick up the rhythm I was playing.

By the fourth time, she would let me move her arms all over the place, varied the speed of her walking and running and had stepped a little rhythmic figure which I utilised; she also started to take hold of me and pull me to the piano.

I did a great deal myself in moving her limbs, lifting her up and lying her down, still singing, hoping she would get the feel of what her body could do, and would then take over and explore for herself. This led to her moving my arms, stepping on and off my lap as I sat on the floor, and clasping me round the neck.

Eventually she let me take her arms wide apart. She could bend her knees when asked, roll backwards and forwards, and explore what she could do with her feet as she lay on the floor, either in relation to the floor or to me. She responded when I spoke to her or called her. As soon as she came to do something herself I not only sang but used percussion, and she played with the percussion instruments also, and would chase me with one of them, and accompany me as I played with cymbals, really picking up the rhythm. And one day as I played she went and moved on her own to the music.

2. *Improvisation to music*

Many people enjoy improvising to music, and find that in doing so they learn unexpected things about themselves. It may be that hearing the music evokes some image or idea, or it may be that some movement is actuated which has never been done before and wasn't even known to be possible, and this can lead to further exploration.

One girl who started with rather fish-like, zig-zag movements, darting here, there and everywhere, developed a beautiful sustained movement which she found most satisfying and greatly extended her vocabulary of movement. On one occasion she and another patient were improvising together to some rather rousing music, and began to mime sword-play, becoming so intense that when they separated in preparation for coming together again, I was prepared to jump in if it became too realistic. But when they did move the first girl when she reached the centre of the room, stopped and drew herself up as though she had become aware of herself, and the dignity that could be hers. At which the whole relationship changed, till it ended with the two with their arms outstretched to one another. This patient said: "I always get something out of the movement session."

Others have played out their problems and sometimes have found a new attitude which they can carry over into their ordinary lives. Still others, despite the fact that when directed they can use their bodies easily and fully, when left to improvise only shuffle round the room. They maintain that in this way they learn a great deal about themselves; such a statement must be treated with the utmost respect and I'm sure it is true. However, there is the possibility that the music stimulates a fantasy and reinforces it, so I think that besides just drifting around to the music there is a need to let the music influence not only thoughts and emotions, but also the body, creating greater physical activity by linking fantasy with a more "down to earth" approach; imagination then begins to function and create. Constantin Stanislavski, in *Stanislavski's Legacy*, edited by E. R. Hapgood (The Bodley Head, 1950, p. 61), is quoted as saying: "In each physical act there is an inner psychological motive, which impels physical action, which expresses its psychic nature." He calls it: "True organic action (inner plus external, psychological plus physical)." Naturally he is speaking of stage performance, but it seems to me to hold good in ordinary living.

Yet the schizophrenic comes to a point where he could begin to return to the world, if he hadn't lost the way. Great skill and co-operation in the therapeutic team is needed to exert the pressure required to enable him to make the break-through, and even patients who have been very resistant show gratitude when such treatment has enabled them to live a normal or near-normal life.

I have seen people moving with beautiful plasticity of body, which conveyed nothing meaningful, only that they were occupied in the achievement of pure bodily movement, even enjoyment seemed absent; and others who obviously had much to express, but were either communicating in such a confused or complicated manner that they were unintelligible, or else were incapable of communication.

When demanding that a patient should work as a whole person, *i.e.* move physically with inner involvement, it must be kept in mind that this is a big demand, which even people who have no psychological problems find difficult to respond to. Though response is extremely personal in all of us, it is no bad discipline to be asked to do something deliberate under guidance.

3. *Self-discovery*

One girl I noticed had a repetitive movement, circling her hands round each other, which was very often accompanied by a flowing, swirling movement of her body. As a movement it was quite pleasant to watch, but the repetition was unusually frequent. I did not comment at first, though from the beginning she was aware of what she did and felt it was significant, although she didn't know how. After some weeks, during which we had worked amongst other things on gliding, direct movements, and hands in particular, she returned again to her own movement. By then the image of a whirlpool had arisen and we used this for a dance sequence—being in a whirlpool. She used the hand-circling with her body withdrawn from her hands, and reproduced the feeling of being taken in the turmoil, then finding that she had come to a rock under her feet, which enabled her to find her balance and push the mud away and down, so that she was able to move in the flow of clear water, and her body took on a straight, dignified, easy gliding posture. She then stopped and said: "That's the first time I have been able to discriminate." I improvised on the piano and gradually we repeated the sequence until we had created a dance.

Another time, I had a young man and a patient accompanying on the piano. He asked me if there was anything I had noticed about his movement, so I asked if there was anything he had discovered; he said that he had found he wasn't very good at flexibility. I knew this man well enough to realise I could let him work directly on all kinds of twisting movement, where with another person I might have gradually come to that. He started moving to the pianist's improvisation and at one point he was drawing circles with his hands in a perfectly direct way. I mentioned I had seen what he was doing, and added: "You seem as though you always want to complete things." He just stared at me and said: "But that's just me, it's been my undoing; how did you know?" I said I hadn't known, I had only observed his movement, and it amazed him that movement could reveal so much. He profited very much from the movement he did, and considerably extended his range, using all he did in a very intelligent way.

CONCLUSIONS

While discussing play, space, and so on I have only touched on some of the ways in which I have worked. I would emphasise that my approach is entirely personal, other people would no doubt use the movement principles quite differently and would not relate them in the manner that I have to the functions of the psyche.

In any case, headings are very limiting, as the moment one begins to write on one aspect, immediately one is involved in others, for movement is a whole, and one can only turn it around and stress one aspect in order to simplify.

Subjects such as aggression are inexhaustible. I feel it is one of the most difficult to understand, and though it exists at all times it seems to be particularly present in this age, demanding attention and action. We have not yet begun to know how to meet it, nor do I pretend I have an answer. I can only describe the way it has happened to come into my work.

Part Two

DRAMA

CHAPTER V

The Use of Drama in Therapy

PLAYING A ROLE

MOVEMENT, dance, mime and drama merge into one another, for any dramatic action involves movement, whether in mime, dance or acting. Drama also comes into our everyday lives in the situations created by our responses to one another. Therefore, in acting a part we can play out our own, or other people's, or imagined, characteristics, emotions and events, either with speech, or without, as in mime or dance.

In playing a role, we are attempting to portray a character in changing moods and emotions and states, sometimes contained within the structure of a play, story or idea, or in the framework of a place, space or stage, in which we are either alone or part of a group.

In such portrayal, excess emotion may be drawn off in the actual playing, or, by being able to sink the personality in the part, a person may contact other people or find a new freedom. Inner problems may be eased temporarily by absorption in the drama, and so may perhaps be seen more objectively by the participant, relieved of the emotional pressure for the time being.

Within the structure of some dramatic situation, particularly when people are at least partly responsible for its creation, they can act out difficulties and learn to adapt through interaction with one another. They have the support of the story or scene, and can learn to fit in with, and get on with, others in its context. One of the main problems of patients is their inability to relate, so to have the chance to experience emotion and speech playing imaginary people may help them to be able to emerge from the shell in which they are imprisoned.

To play in this way demands concentration and involves paying attention to one's surroundings, and this awareness may carry over into ordinary life.

Because movement is inherent in drama, a limber-up is a good way of getting people started, loosening them up and quickening them both mentally and physically. In deciding how to continue, one then has to take into consideration the physical, mental and emotional capabilities of each member of the group, what they want, and what they are prepared to join in.

VARIETY OF ABILITY

Obviously with very deteriorated patients, one is limited, some cannot do much beyond wander about, or walk up and down, apparently little aware of what is going on around them. Yet it is wise not to jump to conclusions, for it is very difficult to know how much they take in. I have been surprised to hear that certain patients, when back in their wards, have taken part in conversations about the drama sessions, which has proved that they have been more alert to the action than has been evident at the time. One is then led to suppose that drama may have more effect on them than has been realised, however remote they may be.

Others are capable of small movements, and get absorbed in doing simple mime. The majority can copy or imitate movement, but find difficulty in initiating anything themselves. To my mind it is very important, and cannot be too often stressed, that a theme should be given which demands something from them, however little, otherwise the movement becomes machine-like, automatic, and meaningless. Many, if asked, can invent some little action which is recognisable by the others, and they like having to guess what another patient is doing. This may be to do with a job, or some happening before their illness. It would seem, then, that they can devise things for themselves.

One man who had been a cabinet-maker was able to mime using a tool very clearly, and to describe what he was doing. Another was holding his hands in such a way that I suggested he might be reading a book. He immediately

62

took up the idea, and when asked what he was reading, answered: "A school book," so that though the idea was given him, he had later interpreted it in his own way. Other patients with more capacity have mimed "arranging flowers" and "dialling and telephoning."

Many patients have difficulty in verbalising, but enjoy mime, and appear to enter into the stories even if they do little, which does bring a relationship to something other than themselves and their own inner world.

IMPROVISATION

A number are very ready to improvise and will welcome what they call "spontaneous acting," which includes impromptu speech, but are loth to repeat anything or work to develop, expand or improve. They like to "express themselves." Quite often, they produce really interesting work, and I am sure such freedom has value. The difficulty lies in the fact that those who find inventing speech and action easy hold the floor, to the exclusion of the more timid and retiring, and so the action tends to become rather diffuse, dissipated and protracted. On the other hand, by being allowed such freedom, some inhibited people begin to come out and find they can act, and sometimes those who feel they cannot join in a movement session enjoy drama, as the emphasis is more on imagery and not so much movement is needed.

It is also very worthwhile if people can be persuaded to polish an improvisation, because it brings a sense of order, gives them the need for perseverance, for discrimination, for repetition, and demands that they work to produce something alive and vital, which can be "spontaneous" in that each time a part is played it has to be created anew in some way. Also there has to be "give and take"—interplay between the characters by adapting the individual part to fit in with the others, or by the whole group acting in unison, so sinking any differences in united action. One of the difficulties is that some patients want more attention than it is possible to give them, and with some this desire is insatiable; but coming into the limelight for a particular speech or line or action, and then having to give place to someone else, can help them over this.

63

WRITING A PLAY

Sometimes a patient will write his own play. The advantage here is that he can use the members of the group for his characterisation, as it is difficult to find a set play which fits all the people concerned. Either there are too many or too few characters, or an unsuitable balance of men and women, and if a suitable play can be found then the contents may be inappropriate. Nevertheless, there is much skill needed to produce dialogue, the unskilled tend to write long speeches, which not only are difficult to memorise but do not give the exchange between people that is desirable. In pruning what is written, devising various ways of putting across the ideas, people again have to adapt to one another.

Many patients have difficulty in memorising, especially those on drugs or undergoing electro-convulsive therapy, but sometimes they can do so by setting and repeating an improvisation until the sentences remain in their minds. It seems that having words coupled with action makes it easier for some to retain the words. Others can achieve the same ends by acting with the book in their hands, though this interferes with their gestures. One girl found she could lose herself in a part in this way and so was enabled to get some relief from her problems, and it brought her into contact with people, which was one of her difficulties; here she had, as it were, a ready-made approach to them.

PLAY-READING

Play-reading, I find, has a limited use; it is enjoyed by some who can only express themselves verbally, and gives them the opportunity to join in a corporate activity, although being static there is not so much give and take. It does impose the discipline of coming in at the right moment, so paying attention to what is going on, and it seems to appeal to those who have literary inclinations.

PRODUCING A PLAY

For those well enough, if a suitable play can be found,

submitting to the work of production is of benefit, and acting can sometimes reach an emotion which is otherwise inaccessible, and can then be experienced and assimilated because it has been brought to light and really looked at. One has to be on the lookout in rehearsal to see how far a person can go in expressing an emotion. He may be able to achieve the result demanded by the part and the producer, but if it is an emotion connected with his problems he may suffer a reversal afterwards if pressed too hard. It is important to gain the consent of the medical authorities beforehand and to work in close collaboration with hospital staff, as there is a risk in such irruptions of problems into consciousness taking place.

Production demands that people relate, adapt and intermingle with each other, and in dealing with the differences, irritations, and squabbles that arise, a preparation for real-life situations can be given.

In performance, there is always the possibility that someone will not be able to meet the demand, or may push himself too far in his loyalty "not to let the side down." It may be possible to foresee that there is such a risk, but such possibilities cannot always be anticipated. If someone suffers a setback by not measuring up to what he has set himself, it may be devastating. Many patients have been brought up to try and live up to a standard of perfection that is beyond their attainment, so that any failure becomes a major tragedy. Yet here we have a chance to discover our own limits and to realise that it is normal not to succeed in all we undertake.

To carry through a performance may, on the other hand, bring a sense of real achievement, and is important for anyone lacking in confidence, for it not only underlines his own self-reliance but shows that he can rely on others as well in playing their parts.

From the foregoing, I hope the importance of observing, assessing and determining how much each patient can attempt has been seen. Usually people of varying ability come together, and then one has to present material which each can use within his own limits.

CHAPTER VI

Drama Group at "Holyrood," South Leigh

INTRODUCTION

THE following is a description of how one drama group started and progressed; it is by no means a model, it simply shows how with one set of patients, working from what they gave me, I attempted to meet the needs of all concerned, which, of course, were constantly fluctuating. Attendance was irregular, though some were very constant as long as they were with us, some left and others joined, so it was a very fluid group.

Our first meeting, and a good many subsequent ones, were in a small room, and this restricted space dictated to a considerable extent what we did. For this reason, instead of starting with a limber-up I suggested the idea of "watching a race." It was possible to line them up so that they could see through the door into darkness; I then said: "Look, they're coming round the bend now," and they all jumped to it, yelling and cheering, which was just what I had hoped for to get their combined attention and concentration. After the initial excitement had died down, of their own accord they carried on improvising a scene of someone having his purse stolen.

Having started at the beginning in this way, I never used a limber-up to start off with these people. If they came in excited then I would give them something quiet, such as "threading a needle" or indicating the size, weight and shape of an object in mime, which would demand a definite focus and detail. Often I just threw it over to them to decide what they would like to do, to see if they could discuss and come to some agreement. Sometimes this worked, but often I had to come in with suggestions, although I tried to draw them out as much as possible to devise their own work.

66

IMPROMPTU ACTING

"Spontaneous acting" was what they all wanted. I would rather use the word "impromptu," for at times the acting was very laboured and the ideas by no means "spontaneous." Spontaneity implies for me an upspringing without conscious or external volition, which gives life, and can be part of improvisation, or equally well can vitalise what has already been created and worked on. Peter Slade maintains it can be guided (*op. cit.*, p. 1), but lays stress on the fact that true spontaneity may be guided by only suggesting what to do, without showing how to do it, though in some cases, particularly in the beginning, one has to show how to do an action, too; but one should work towards self-reliance and responsible creation by individuals as soon as possible. However, this isn't to say that there are no moments, flashes of true spontaneity in "impromptu" acting, even when laboured.

On this first occasion, having used the stimulation of the "race," I took up the group's idea of an impromptu scene and they chose "On Brighton Beach."

Immediately, people volunteered to play parts. A child, her mother and spinster aunt, a deck-chair attendant, a jelly-fish, a deaf holidaymaker with a radio, a beach warden, a quiet lady and an ice-cream vendor.

The first three came in followed by the deck-chair attendant, and there was play between them over deck-chairs and bathing, while the others appeared. The jelly-fish swam around and eventually stung the child and was chased away. Meanwhile the quiet lady complained to the beach warden about the radio, and finally the ice-cream vendor caused a diversion.

Everyone talked at the same time and it was a bit of a melée. I persuaded them to repeat it, and though there was objection on the grounds that it wouldn't be spontaneous, they agreed to try.

Normally, in a large room, the different scenes can go on quite happily at the same time, in fact it is important that this should happen, each little group inventing their own speech and action. At other times, alternation of groups and characters gives everyone a turn at being the centre of interest which, as I have said before, enables the more inhibited to be brought forward, and helps those who are always in the fore-front to give way to others.

For such improvisation, I found it helpful if the subject chosen were familiar to all, so each could contribute to the plot, otherwise it was difficult to include everyone.

One of the subjects the group elected to try was "drug peddling," at a time when drug addition was not so much in the news. They decided on a café scene, in which the drugs were to be handed over by a pusher. But they were at a loss as to how to do it, and some of the "customers" sitting at the café tables were reluctant to join in. A row developed in the play between two or three people over the service, which was quite unconnected with the theme, and was not woven in, so nothing held together.

At the group's request, we had a repetition, and though it was still a bit slipshod they devised an ending, where two innocent ladies were hauled off by a policeman for interrogation, which was quite amusing.

Despite the fact that it didn't really come off, it was an interesting attempt and showed the need for greater clarity of design, of entrances and exits, and it certainly highlighted how two people could run away with a plot, causing it to fall to pieces. I could have stepped in and organised but I felt more would be discovered if I left them to find out. It wasn't as though we were trying to produce anything. They also realised how difficult it was to make a character convincing.

CHARACTERISATION

Our next step was to play with ideas of how to build up a character.

To start with, we made out slips of paper each with the description of a character on it, which were drawn by pairs of people who then had to invent a dialogue or mime between them. We had such combinations as a gypsy and a South African farmer, a commercial traveller and an irate member of a Ratepayers' Association, a schoolgirl and a colonial bishop retired to write his memoirs.

I was amazed at what was produced, as there was real interplay of dialogue and action between the characters,

68

however incompatible. In each case they made a relationship.
With some people, it is possible to practise specific ways of
moving in character:

1. Walking in an imaginary costume, *e.g.* a Greek tunic,
   a dress of a particular period with a very full skirt, a
   suit of armour, a dress with a train, knee breeches,
   embroidered waistcoat and lace cuffs, a cloak.
2. Breaking it down to footwear or headgear, *e.g.* sandals,
   high boots, gumboots, shoes with long pointed toes,
   high heels, moccasins, a topper, an Ascot creation, a
   sombrero, a wimple, a wig, a perruque, helmets—from
   steel to balaclava—bonnets.

The texture of a garment affects movement by the variation
in weight—a tulle veil as compared to a Pompadour wig, the
long, full brocade or woollen skirt of an Elizabethan lady as
opposed to the silks and muslins of the Empire style. The
constriction or freedom of a costume also affects movement,
as in the corseted Victorian miss, or the present-day tennis
player.

An experienced actor can convey all these clothes simply
by the way he moves.

STIMULATING THE INVENTION OF A CHARACTER

Suggesting a situation such as:

1. "You are sitting alone or with one or more people in the
evening, and you hear a noise outside. Who are you? How
do you react?"

The following are some of the results I have seen.

(*a*) Two women waiting for and welcoming a visitor.
(*b*) Two old women winding wool, getting very angry with
     one another, are frightened by a noise, one takes the
     poker, goes and opens the door, where she is accosted
     by a man, whom she bribes to go away.
(*c*) A pair, frightened by the noise, on opening the door
     find it is caused by torrential rain.

2. One person can be asked to start a scene as a character,

69

then involve another person, who in turn brings in someone else, and so on until all are included.

One very quiet girl chose to be a woman starting in labour, telling a neighbour, who took her to hospital and involved in turn, nurses, doctor, etc. and the scene developed into a Caesarian operation and the result—triplets.

A variation is for the first person to start playing and the rest to decide how they could join in, doing so when they feel the opportunity occurs.

3. Throw out an idea, *e.g.* Christmas Pudding, the Gas Man, shopping, genius.

"The Gas Man" produced a spirited conversation between the man who had come to mend the Ascot, and penetrated to the bathroom where a lady was having a bath, but quite unperturbed they engaged in talk while he mended the Ascot, impervious to the cries of a child returning hurt from school!

4. Arrange an imaginary set, each person memorising exactly where each piece of furniture is said to be, and then ask for a scene to be invented which could be played in that setting.

One such scene was: an aspidistra, a glass-topped table containing knick-knacks, sofa, table, chairs. It was rather interesting that the emotion conveyed was what depicted the characters: concern over upsetting a bowl of water when washing the aspidistra, or breaking a trayful of tea things, some calmly repairing the damage, others getting in a state; distress over handling objects from the glass-topped table which aroused painful memories; delight on finding a lost necklace among the cushions on the sofa; happiness and anger over the reading of a letter.

CHAPTER VI.

Mime and Speech

MIME

I HAVE referred several times to mime, and particularly to its value for those who cannot verbalise. So much can be conveyed without speech, and to find a means of communication in such a way facilitates making relationship.

Often it is discovered how lax we are in observation. When asked to mime "sewing," people frequently fail to realise that after putting the needle into the material one has to let go and take hold of the other end to draw the thread through, and instead they do a scooping movement as though holding the needle all the time.

When attention is paid to doing such small practical things, by making people more aware and interested in the quality of movement required and how different parts of the body are used, they can become aware of themselves, and then when relating to outside things it becomes easier to do the ordinary practical things of life. Quite often handling an actual object and then doing the same action in mime makes for greater clarity. Then the size, weight and surface of the object is felt, and adaptation made accordingly. For instance, trying different sizes of flower-pots, some full of earth, some empty, feeling the rough surface—and then drying a wine-glass with its delicacy and smooth, slippery quality. Trying to reproduce the same actions without the object can show how we change the elements of our movements. If then we can take this into handing someone an imaginary piece of china, the attitude to that person is also conveyed in the movement, and this is important if portraying a character.

Concerted action can also be a way of relating. Imagine

71

moving a grand piano. This needs several people, it has to be visualised, its exact place in space allocated, its size and weight and shape assessed to determine how to approach and handle it. Then each person has to adjust his own body in relation to the others, and together they use their bodies with the necessary physical energy and posture and inner intention, even though they have no tangible object.

Asking individuals to produce their own mime, however simple, gives them scope for creativity. One patient (*see* Fig. 14) showed us "catching a small feather, smoothing it and blowing it away." It was so effective that we could almost see and feel the lightness, and airiness, and softness as she smoothed it and let it go, and her own appreciation of such a lovely little thing was in her action. This is true participation and absorption, and being watched is part of the action and not outside observation.

People can get together and produce their own mime. It is as well to limit the time they have for discussion beforehand, as they tend to argue endlessly, and it is useful to allow time for them to see each other's work. If they have to guess and make their mime so clear that it can be guessed, they seem to forget about being watched. I think this is because the people watching are, in fact, participating. The guessing game can also be used by giving a subject and then one or more give their own interpretation for the others to guess. One patient interpreted "losing something" as "lost reputation," played tragically, very quietly and so well that the guess was "loss of a good name."

Mime can be repeated with speech, or alternatively after performing a scene with speech it can be repeated in mime alone, and often it becomes apparent how little we know about how we move even in the ordinary actions of daily life.

Practising different ways of approaching people, and the ways in which we do this, shows how the small subtleties in movement affect others, and many patients are quite oblivious that their approach may be the cause of someone reacting negatively; so often they blame the other person, which in fact we all do.

We all know how we feel when being served with a cup of tea which is slapped down in front of us, the contents spilling

Fig. 14 Playing with a feather

73

over. How many of us are aware of things that we have not experienced ourselves? For instance, a patient's reactions to having a wound dressed—some dressers so deft and neat and gentle that they cause a minimum of pain, others stripping off the dirty dressings strongly and suddenly without any idea of what they are doing.

In mime, it is possible to see and feel what we are doing ourselves; naturally with patients one has to be careful how one approaches such work. But as many of them have difficulties in communication and relationship, to mime, paying attention to the detail of what they are doing, may help them in their attitude to other people.

SPEECH

With some patients, it is possible to work at actual speech training, and some have fun with tongue-twisters, poetry, short verses and words said with differences of inflection expressing varying meanings and emotions.

1.   Simple situations and emotions can be made very pointed by gestures instigated by a word or sentence:
     "Here."
     "Now."

2.   Entrances and exits with speech can also be used for precision, timing and dramatic effect:
     "Stop! Stop! There's been a landslide."
     "Hail, my loyal subjects."
     "I go to meet my fate."
     "Let me go!"

The suddenness of bursting in or breaking away (*see* Fig. 15), as in the first and last examples, enables some tongue-tied people to utter. In making such a greeting as the second sentence, the entry, to be effective, has to be made with "presence," which can give a sense of being a person.

It is important to know patients before giving them such sentences to play individually, as the sentences need to be prepared according to the personal problems, not simply to make them play them out but to canalise their feelings. Some

74

Fig. 15 Bursting in with exciting news

sentences can be used by each in turn, and then differences in interpretation become interesting.

While exploring entrances and exits, the management of a door or a curtain or even a screen can be practised in a similar way. One person can sit, while another comes in silently and surprises him, the patients inventing their own situations.

A door can be thrown open and an entry made

    (*a*) ushering in an important personage with a retinue,
    (*b*) bursting in with exciting news.

Such simple themes give great scope for imagination and invention.

SENTENCES

Those who cannot carry through a set part can often build a scene round a given sentence, with one or more people:

"I can't do it, I'm terrified of heights—I tell you I can't do it!"

"Quick throw a blanket round her! Hurry—hurry!"

"Arthur, how much longer is this lecture going to last? I'm getting hungry."

Sometimes sentences can deal with a single emotion, *e.g.* "I feel very angry," or the sentence can be one that requires a response from the other person, *e.g.* "I'm very angry with you."

Sometimes expressing an emotion deliberately may be a means of canalising, but I would never choose an actual situation between people for them to act, that, I think, would be asking for trouble. I have, however, had two people work out their hostility to one another during a movement session, without discussing it at the time. I didn't know till long afterwards that there was this relationship, and that it had got to the point that they couldn't even speak to one another, and so I gave them a theme where they had to relate to another person. These two started straight off sparring, but gradually they played it out, and we went on to a mime in which they joined, and at the end of the session they were able to discuss their feelings with one another, and found that their attitude had changed, and remained so.

PLAYS

One patient wrote a short play about a travel agency which needed constant adaptation to the players, and we then realised the difficulties of writing suitable dialogue. The constant change-over of patients and their varied capacities meant we couldn't really produce a play, but though this was frustrating it was an interesting experience and gave a good many people an outlet for their energies and talents.

We produced and performed one play only, which went very well, and some gained confidence in the achievement, having never imagined they could act. One in "loyalty to the side," though she had the most dramatic talent and carried through the evening, had a negative period afterwards, but this may not have been altogether due to the play, as she had such recurrent times.

Some, who for one reason or another, weren't able to act (one was a nun who at that time had no dispensation to allow her to take part in acting) got satisfaction from being stage-manager, and in one play the stage-manager was used to change the scenes.

When rehearsing a play, if this gets sticky, it can help to drop the script and start improvising on the situation. When taking up the script again, it has a renewed freshness and possibly an upsurge of spontaneity results.

ROLE-PLAYING

I distinguish role-playing from psycho-drama, which I consider should only be undertaken with the co-operation of a psychotherapist, but role-playing is an aspect of drama, as anyone playing a character is in fact playing a role.

Frequently patients will choose a role which has a direct bearing on their difficulties, though they may not realise this, but do so more in the way a child identifies himself with different people in his play—he becomes in turn, hero, father, king, or heroine, mother, queen (if a girl), and the drama develops as it goes along.

The patient does not deliberately set the scene of some past event, but by acting different roles he may play out what he was never able to achieve as a child in play or imagination, or he may invent a role where he is put in the position he finds difficult.

As an example, one man evolved a scene where a performer, playing a comic part, finding he is unable to make his audience laugh, enlists the help of some children who, though at first suspicious, end by dressing him differently, thus enabling him to communicate and so amuse.

In such a scene, a patient can have a subjective creative experience, but he also needs to view what he does objectively, in order to help himself to find a new attitude. In the scene quoted, the chief character made a forward outgoing move in asking the children's help, and I think it was significant that

77

they were cast as children. We didn't know how they would react, in fact they eyed him, sizing him up, and were rather sarcastic and amused at his dilemma, but in the end responded to his appeal. In these roles, the patients did not have to try and act a particular person, so inviting the remark: "Well, of course, my brother (or sister) was never like that" but were free to face the chief character with any rejoinder, which might just as well have been a rebuff. In making a forward gesture, or taking a rebuff in play, it can then become possible to do so in actuality.

CHAPTER VIII

Pilot Study for a Research Project Undertaken by "Sesame"

INTRODUCTION

THE ways of working just described would be suitable for patients of a certain intelligence who could use their imagination and invention to create for themselves. Yet it is possible to reach people of very varying ability through drama.

Every person who attempts to work in a therapeutic situation needs to have his knowledge, experience, techniques and understanding at his finger-tips, to be drawn on when and where appropriate.

Even though it is necessary to plan before taking a group, one must be ready to discard all one has prepared. Yet possible situations and problems and ways of meeting them may be considered beforehand, and one can think out material that might come in, provided one keeps an open mind. One cannot work by rule of thumb if one is really going to draw these people out. One has to work from the patients and their needs and not from fixed ideas.

One experiment in which I participated was carried out at Goodmayes Hospital under the clinical direction of a Principal Psychologist with Drama training, and I was extremely fortunate in having some of a "Sesame" group experienced in performing mime to audiences of handicapped people and then getting them to join in. The rest came because of their concern for such people.

"Sesame," recognised by the Department of Health and Social Security, is an organisation working to promote movement and drama with the mentally or physically sick or handicapped and the elderly.

"Sesame" arranges demonstrations (under professional direction) by two groups, who perform in order gradually to involve the audience in active participation and encourage those working or interested in the field to undertake training provided by "Sesame" in workshops, courses and conferences.

"Sesame" also undertakes research projects under scientific control in co-operation with the staff of hospitals and other centres.

"Sesame" was founded and is directed by Mrs. Marian Lindkvist.

FORMATION OF THE GROUP

The patients selected were long-stay schizophrenics who had made little or no response to other methods of treatment. They were socially withdrawn and many were thought disordered. A few patients who were less chronic were included because we thought they might help the others, but they soon lost interest because the activities were below the level of their ability. If we scaled the work to the differing abilities, then certain people took prominence and the others tagged on in a crowd, whereas what we wanted was for each patient, however remote, to have some place in the action.

HOW THE DRAMA GROUP WAS USED

Initially, we began with the drama group limbering up and performing a mime, then the patients were encouraged and helped to participate. The approach was modified as treatment progressed because the patients were on their feet at the beginning and it was necessary actively to involve them from the start otherwise they withdrew and further participation was difficult to achieve. In order to sustain the patients' interest it was necessary for the drama group to improvise according to the patients' needs. Thus we had to develop a new approach, depending on each member of the drama group being able to improvise, and using what they were doing all the time to stimulate patients to take part. They organised small groups and if, for some reason or other, one group was slower than the others, they continued inventing as they went along to enable the one group to catch up, or while a problem was sorted out. They also assisted patients with their roles.

The drama group was not used to improvising in this way, but they were so competent and sensitive to the patients that they soon developed this way of working, which gave them opportunity to talk with the patients, especially if any became at all upset. In view of this development we rarely performed, and in any case time for rehearsal became too difficult to arrange.

THE GENERAL WORK OF THE PATIENTS

I always started with a limber-up for these patients either on a movement or a mime theme, and the withdrawn ones responded best to movement both mentally and physically.

Practically all could copy or imitate, though in everything I tried to leave opportunity for them to do something of their own, and if one produced some variation I would try and use it in what we were doing.

Having found previously that very sick patients worked well in a circle holding hands, I started in this way, and continued whenever we were a small enough number. With a large number the room was not suited to making a satisfactory circle. If they divided into two circles I could keep neither contact nor adequate observation. Because of this we used two straight lines of patients each partnered by a member of staff or drama group, for initially the patients were unable to work with each other. Some formation was necessary for the limbering-up because the confusion or disorientation of most of the patients rendered the usual freedom of movement impractical.

One of the problems in all hospitals is that interested staff, apart from those involved in the group, want to come in to watch, but are too shy to join in. This often disturbs the therapists' and patients' concentration and some withdraw from active participation. At Goodmayes it was finally decided that only visitors willing to take part should be admitted. At such times, it was most noticeable that everyone was involved and patients did not drift away; in fact, the patients enjoyed strangers coming in and taking part, and could include them.

Quite apart from anything else, the leader requires the least amount of distraction, for he not only has to observe and direct, but needs to be in touch with everything that is happening all over the room at any one time and has to be ready to develop or change the action as need arises, and to have foresight in order to decide what to do next. If there is no member of staff present who can take clinical responsibility for the patients, the work of the leader is complicated by having to make sure that no disturbed patient who should be under continual observation slips away unnoticed.

The great need is to meet people where they are, and many are very confused and living in a dark world of fantasy, sometimes pleasant, often terrifying. I find that to turn the lights low at times gives an extension of this inner world in which they exist, and into which they can risk entering. Because of the dimness they do not feel exposed, and then they may find that this world overlaps the outside world; in the dimness they contact others and find that it is not too frightening, and then by degrees they can come out into greater consciousness with the increase of light. Twilight can be a bridge, and can be a place where we relate to their inner world from which they can develop a greater contact with reality, although care has to be taken that those who are very withdrawn or disturbed are not frightened by others larking about under cover of the lack of light.

Most withdrawn patients move in a constricted way, and one would think that they were not very aware of other people, but if one of the drama group were absent patients would notice, and some would say: "Where's So-and-so?"

One or two of the group, having made a contact with a patient, would work with him most of the evening, but though the patient was greatly helped at the time, if that person were prevented from coming it had a bad effect. In an attempt to avoid this we decided to change about more frequently, so that this dependence on one person did not occur.

I have tried to outline the problems that may be met with, but the method of dealing with them often needs much adaptation. Reports from psychiatrists and nurses and psychological assessments indicated that many of the patients were less withdrawn and uncommunicative after nine months' treatment. Most of them were more sociable and less emotionally flat. Patients enjoyed attending, and some stated that it was the event they looked forward to during the week more than any other.

The type of work undertaken included eight scenes and one dance that were rehearsed beforehand, mostly performed by the drama group before involving the patients.

The Ugly King	Fire Scene
The Ice-Cream Vendor	Happy and Broken Families
Forest Scene	The Milk-bottle
Giant Scene	The Arrival of the Film-Star
	War Dance

Twenty scenes were partially rehearsed, but were built up together with the patients. One patient, we found, had taught in a dancing-school, so we made a scene round her as the teacher.

We also used a number of scenes from ordinary life:

Coach Trip	The Lost Key of the Canteen
Underground Train	Apple-picking
Packing a Parcel	Moving House
Birthday Party	The Postman
	The Hole in the Road

These terms are self-explanatory.

We found the sense of occasion, the dignity of royalty, processions and doing homage evoked real participation in solemnity, ceremony, respect and veneration as well as rejoicing, in such scenes as Rehearsal for a Coronation, King Arthur and his Court (*see* Fig. 16), the Princess and her Suitors.

Anything to do with eating and drinking was enjoyed, and everyone would join in. On the occasion of a scene in a café a patient said: "It makes you feel quite hungry." In a bar scene, one man said he would have a "cherry-brandy," and another time "whisky and vodka." Three weeks later, he referred to the latter, saying he didn't think it would be a very nice drink.

After a scene depicting climbing over a wall the same man

Fig. 16   Doing homage at King Arthur's court

said how fascinated he had been in the way the group gave the impression of getting up and over the wall, by simultaneously raising themselves and lowering their hands.

It is difficult to comment on remarks made by patients as, out of context, they may seem pointless, whereas at the time they could be really significant, showing that the patients were aware of people and their surroundings, and were using observation and their imagination and not just fantasying. They noticed individual members of the drama group in such phrases as: "You're looking nice to-day," "You're wearing a different pullover," "What's it like to be short like you?" One, when asked why he laughed, said: "You amuse me." They would discuss clothes and cooking, and what they had

84

been doing, and one girl wrote out a recipe from which a member of the group made a dish and brought it to show her.

One girl always wanted to know our names, and an autistic boy, who we were told did not talk on the wards, except to his mother when she visited, developed to a point where he could talk to each of us in turn; when one of the group brought a map he would look up the places and he began to hold conversations with several members.

One of them said: "I like happy endings like this." Another, having invented a whole mime about an office, said: "This is just pretend."

Another, acting the part of a princess, gave a detailed description of the dress she was imagining she wore; she was a girl who usually joined in the more active work, and said: "I like the exercises."

Two women were heard to say to each other: "Is this acting?" "It's all imagining." "That's what we need."

In the apple-picking scene, one of the group mimed falling off a ladder and a patient immediately went to her assistance, while another was only concerned about his wages which he said he was going to use for his fares.

In these instances, it was quite plain that the patients were aware of what they were doing, but sometimes when talking with them it was difficult to distinguish between fact and fantasy.

One man for a long time would not join in, and said: "I'll be allowed to join in when I can behave." In the end, he got enthused by the "War Dance." He was at times very noisy and had a very quick rhythm, sometimes dancing as though he were doing a Spanish dance. At first working on his own, he later began to join in and contributed definite ideas, his rhythm became quieter and he began to move in a sustained way. He often made a variation of his own in the limber-up which was picked up and used by me with everybody. In the end he improved very much, and his general behaviour was markedly affected.

When asked to mime a character, patients would choose for themselves, and the following are a few of their choices:

A mother holding her baby (*see* Fig. 17)

Fig. 17   How to hold a baby

A ballet-dancer
A skater
A housewife putting a lace curtain on an expanding wire

Those who couldn't choose a role could be persuaded to mime playing ball, darts, football or to do some occupational action such as washing-up, turning a tap, using a tool, mending a leak, pouring a drink, and so on.

Working as partners, mostly one drama group member and one patient, they mimed:

86

An invalid being helped	Stroking a sheepdog
A naughty child teasing an adult	Riding a tandem
Washing up	Driving a Covent Garden lorry

Unpacking a Christmas parcel

These are ways in which patients worked with the drama group, and I hope these examples may be of use in indicating a line which might be followed. Even the very withdrawn would respond to a remark; they paid attention to what was going on even if not actually taking part, and some could use their imagination and yet distinguish the real from the "pretend."

Part Three

RELAXATION AND RELATIONSHIP

CHAPTER IX

Relaxation

THE FUNCTION OF RELAXATION

How often people say to us: "Re-*lax*." A little word so easily spoken and such good advice!

But just to be told to relax surely doesn't help, unless we can do so at will. Anyway, what do they mean when they say "relax"? Possibly we know at heart they are right; if we did relax we could ease up, not be in such a rush, not get so hot and bothered, take things as they come, and so on. Yet we feel annoyed because they give us no indication of how to achieve a relaxed attitude. So we continue in a state of tension, meeting every eventuality in a taut, strained manner, tightening up at any uncertainty or unpleasantness.

But clearly, our very life depends on the alternation of tension and relaxation in the systole and diastole of the heart and the inspiration and expiration of the lungs; it is this rhythm between opposites to which we owe our continued existence.

The physiological aspect of these subconscious functions is complex, but it is simple to see that there are frequent changes in the speed of the action of the heart and lungs according to the amount of energy we require in carrying out a task, yet that the rhythm of the opposites is maintained.

Tension has become something of a dirty word, yet some tension is necessary in the strength we have to use to perform certain actions. If we pick up an object we often grip it unnecessarily tightly, so using a greater degree of strength than required, and sometimes we retain the strength when the need for it is past. It is important to be able to recognise these causes of tension.

How often we use more energy than is needed to accomplish what we set out to do! If we were more aware of the interplay between tension and relaxation and the enormous range of degree in increase and decrease, we could adjust our activity and conserve our strength, and so not build up unnecessary tension.

Watch a skilled labourer on a farm, and see the way he has found a rhythm which enables him to continue working

Fig. 18   Sitting at a desk

for hours on end. I remember reading, in Adrian Bell's book *Corduroy* (first published in 1930 by Cobden Sanderson), his description of his first attempt at lifting beet, and how exhausted he became until he caught the rhythm of picking the beet from the ground, chopping the leaves off and throwing it in the wagon. A man who went to a doctor feeling really ill, after examination was asked about his job, and it transpired that he had to lean forward to do it, in the way that many of us sit at a desk (*see* Fig. 18). The advice he was given was periodically to lean back and really stretch for a few seconds (*see* Fig. 19), since his entire trouble came from the constriction caused by leaning forward, which inhibited the flow of blood so that the nerves never got nourished, and muscles and ligaments remained static and lost their elasticity.

In factories in some countries and in workshops for the physically-handicapped, it is customary to give breaks for at least a change of position and sometimes exercises.

Fig. 19 Stretching

93

HOW TENSIONS ARISE

Tensions arise not only through the way we pursue physical actions, but through our attitudes, emotions, feelings and thoughts reacting on our physical impulses.

We all know the type of man who defeats his own object by driving himself until he drops; he has allowed himself no time to let up, to recover, unaware of the need that to maintain the rhythm of life there must be an opposite—shall we call it work and play? By play I don't mean necessarily going off to play golf or cricket or tennis, though I'm all for people using their leisure for games and sport. No, I mean play in the sense of freedom, of light-heartedness, which should be used even momentarily, to keep the rhythm.

Of course, there are occasions when we need tension, we have to brace ourselves to meet or cope with certain events and the mind and body adjust accordingly. But often our trouble is that we don't pay attention to the opposite. We don't take the small opportunities, even in situations when we could relax briefly, to give ourselves a breathing-space.

Fear, anxiety, panic and apprehension, mistrust and suspicion also cause tension, through physical changes which enable us to meet crises when they arise. Normally, when the crisis is over and the fear or other emotion eases, the body returns to its normal state. There are, however, times when the fear or suspicion, or whatever it is, is prolonged and with it the tension, and so the whole rhythm of living is disturbed.

Again, a child may be subjected to stresses and strains in early life which are beyond its capacity to bear, and the emotions get repressed; in doing so, a state of tension is started which may increase until, in later life, the pressure from the unconscious of all this repressed material becomes too great and breakdown ensues.

Many other causes may be behind excessive tension, preventing any possibility of relaxation. Naturally if the cause can be brought to light and either resolved or removed, or we can learn to live with some conditions, then relaxation is an automatic result, or at least it can be. But often a habit has been formed which has to be gradually unlearned, like a tangled skein which has to be unravelled. It is at this point, while the psychological aspect is being treated, that it can help to work physically through the body to find an easy relation between tension and relaxation.

All through the ages people have devised ways of working with the body, some drastic, some as simple as the advice given to Naaman in the Bible to go and wash in the River Jordan. Some find one way is a help and some use other means.

REALISATION OF TENSION AND WAYS OF RELEASE

Though we may be aware of being tense, we may be unaware of where our tensions lie, and we may be in such a state that as we begin to relax we find other tensions we didn't know of and we experience exhaustion. Often people do not wish to continue because they say it makes them tired; only if they work through this stage can they come to any degree of freedom, and some can be persuaded to persevere.

To find out where we are tense, we have to become aware of the different parts of our bodies, and to realise the tension in each part; this bodily awareness is an essential in learning to relax.

To some people, the ability to relax means simply allowing the body to become completely limp, but often when people then start to move again all the old tensions return.

According to Flack (in Schilder, *op. cit.*, p. 208): "Every change in the psychic attitude provokes a change in the dynamic situation as a whole, experienced as specific sequences in muscular tension and relaxation in expressive movement. Tension is connected with the feeling or the display of energy; conversely, the loosening of tension and relaxation of muscle are connected with loss of energy, and with the sensation of heaviness in different parts of the body."

Have you ever watched a cat jump up to a window on hearing a dog bark? Keen, taut, eager, trembling with tension in its excitement, until either its curiosity is satisfied or its fear allayed, it will soften gradually and eventually return to where it was sleeping, and either start to wash or settle down again to sleep. When a cat is gloriously content, lying stretched out in front of a fire, it is really flaccid, and at times will allow itself to be picked up in that state. At other times if stroked it will gradually stretch and purr with pleasure.

The difference between displaying energy and letting it go is clearly felt if an arm or a leg or a head is lifted by another person to see if the weight of that part can really be given up. If the feeling of letting go is not experienced or there is not sufficient confidence in the other person, the tension will be sustained and the weight not released. When the tension is released then the limb or head becomes very heavy to hold.

Patients can test this for themselves by lifting one arm with the opposite hand and holding the weight of that arm until they feel it as heavy as possible. They can do the same standing, lifting a leg with both hands under the thigh and letting go the hands, when the leg will drop to the floor; again they will feel the difference in weight when really given up.

If you watch a ballerina during a lift you can plainly see the way she carries some of her own weight by her control, she suits her strength to the occasion, and using tension very purposefully every muscle plays a part in that control. Ideally, relaxation is using the requisite amount of energy, the right degree of tension, for whatever is undertaken, varying as the situation changes.

Very often the easiest way for people to relax is to lie on the floor with the feet apart, with hands on the diaphragm and fingers slightly apart, or arms thrown out loosely sideways from the shoulder to lie along the floor just below shoulder level. It is essential to have a rug for each person to lie on, as the very act of being still in that position can cause the body to cool down to some extent. A second rug to cover can be provided if needed. I find it best to have the curtains drawn; I have tried all ways, but the dimness aids the concentration and attention both for my class and me, and it is useful to have people in a similar position as long as I am giving directions.

The mood and ability of members of the group dictate the approach, but in such a quiescent class it is even more important to have some idea of the working of the body, and the various things that can go wrong with it, for usually the people who come to relaxation have more physical troubles than those who come to movement.

1. *Lying on the floor*

Some people have an aversion to lying on the floor; it has some very deep symbolical meaning for them. Going down may mean going into the unconscious, and in order for them not to be overwhelmed they should not be expected to work on the floor, or even towards the floor, until the time arrives when they can risk it. Some feel the floor is dirty, and they may have an obsession about cleanliness. I never force anyone who has such an aversion, but sometimes they can be persuaded or gently eased towards trying it for themselves in their own way.

When lying on the floor, the first thing is to become aware of the contact with it, and I often ask people to discover which part of their bodies they can feel touching the floor; everyone is built differently, so some may find they touch in more places than others.

The floor can also be experienced as a secure support, so sometimes I suggest they think of the floor and its stability, that they won't be let down, and then feel that they can sink right on to it and be held.

I always start with the feet and work upwards as I have found this satisfactory. So many people complain of "being up in my head" and this concentration on the feet seems to release the circulation and nerves of the whole body; maybe it also prevents any rush of blood to the head.

2. *The basic movement principles and relaxation*

I adapt and invent to suit the needs of individuals and newcomers without losing sight of the needs of everyone else. Even so, often specific difficulties arise, by reason of past injury or habit or body shape, which have to be taken into consideration. I use the basic movement principles as well as just lying and attempting to let go. Tension and relaxation can be thought of in terms of strength and lightness and suddenness and sustainment, and used in this way by gripping and releasing each part in turn. To start with, the action should be done quickly so as not to tire the nerves. Increase and decrease and acceleration and deceleration can also come in.

People should be encouraged to find out for themselves

whether they have relaxed or just stretched in another direction
or wriggled! For example, you can tell patients to "make a
fist" and then ask them to relax their hand. Many of them will
then extend their fingers till the palm is taut. You can then
point out that this is not relaxation but is merely producing
an opposite tension, whereas in true relaxation the fingers will
curl loosely as the tension goes and control is released. They
should learn to observe that there is a difference between this
and deliberately curling the fingers.

Pressing isolated parts of the body against the floor and
letting go is another way of using the opposites of tension and
relaxation, which can be done from the feet up, including the
back of the head. In fact, the latter is important because it is
one way of releasing the muscles from the neck up behind the
ears and to the base of the skull. Parts can be raised a few
inches off the floor and let drop to test how relaxed they are:
heels, knees, seats, elbows and shoulders in turn.

Another way of testing is by bringing the knee over the
chest, dropping a foot on the floor so that it is just supported,
then giving a little push to the foot, which lets the whole leg
slide out completely floppy.

The face tends to be very tense. Sometimes people find it a
help to smooth their faces with their own hands, from the
centre of the forehead towards the temples, from either side of
the nose across the cheeks to meet the ears, drawing the hands
downwards and dragging the jaw open as they go. Make a
game of it, play with the idea that it makes one look very
stupid, as some people are very afraid of making faces. Yet to
be able to do so is another way of gaining freedom. Working
on the spatial idea of narrow and wide, get them to draw in
their faces towards their noses, and then let go, or to spread
them out like a sun and then let go, or push their lips forwards
forming a snout. The mouth, too, can be stretched or contracted and released.

Some people are so ill at ease in their bodies that they have
little or no sense of the individual parts; they cannot even feel
that a foot or hand is touching the floor, nor if they raise one
and drop it can they feel it as it drops back. Some cannot
move their shoulders, they may move their chests instead, and
have no realisation that they have done so. If they can bear

to be touched, they may feel the warmth of a hand but may not be able to locate it. They can describe a part but have no sensation in it. Sometimes if they can come to feel one part then it can be used to relate feeling to another part. There are probably hidden fears and insecurity or aggression in this situation, which it is very important to be able to recognise. If one produces too sudden a relaxation it might be devastating, as it would break through the withdrawal too abruptly.

People who have not been able to relax or who have recoiled from touch, may have a great desire to relate and communicate. One aim should be to find a means through which they can become more aware in their bodies. I have described earlier where the use of the piano led one patient to become conscious of her hands, and to realise that they were constantly doing other things for her, such as picking up a kettle or handling art materials. They became her friends, as she herself expressed it, and so could be used to become aware of other parts and eventually of her whole person.

CHAPTER X

Relationship

IMPORTANCE OF RELATIONSHIP

THERE is a great deal of talk these days about relationship, but it seems to me that we understand less and less what it really is or how to achieve it. Yet in any therapeutic situation, some relationship is vital if the patient and those caring for him are to co-operate in order to create the conditions in which the healing process, the "vis medicatrix naturae" can function.

When a patient is very sick in mind or body he is forced to shelve all responsibility for himself because he is incapable of consciously co-operating, therefore those who look after him have to take the responsibility for a time—he is dependent on them. But there comes a moment when they need to get in touch with him in order to help him to help himself. They are the preparers of the pathway back to normal living. For this reason, they need to have every possible means of making relationship at their disposal.

Patients, because of their vulnerability, insecurity, fear and anxiety, tend to build a protective wall between themselves and other people; or the very nature of their illness can be a barrier. Some appear prickly, irritable, explosive, or bear a "don't touch me" aspect, though inwardly they may be crying out to be reached.

Some very withdrawn patients give no hint that they are aware of what is going on around them. An assistant matron at a psychiatric hospital once told me that she had taken a group of country dancers into a ward of chronics. As far as she could see while they were there no one took the slightest notice of them, but she said afterwards she never went into

100

that ward without someone saying: "When are you going to bring your girls again, Matron?"

We are inclined to dub such people "cabbages," and indeed this may be true of some; but these people, at any rate, though appearing completely inert, by making a response eventually— and a verbal response at that—proved that they were more alive than was thought. Which makes one wonder how much more we could relate in non-verbal ways were we more aware of how we look, appear and move, as well as speak. Even in speech we often do not realise the tone of voice we use, and how it affects the people around us.

TRAINING OF AWARENESS BETWEEN PARTNERS

Veronica Sherborne has made a film called "In Touch" which is about students in training to teach mentally-handicapped children. The film shows them working individually, in partners and in their own group, then each with one child, and finally one with a group of children, learning to use movement with them. In her note on the film, Veronica Sherborne says:

> "A student can only teach or communicate what she herself has experienced, so, getting used to the idea that her body can be an expressive instrument and developing her kinaesthetic sense are extremely important to her."

The film stresses the training of awareness and sensitivity both in body and voice, and it is quite plain how the training enables the students to communicate with, and to help, these children.

After all, these bodies of ours are our only means of communication. It is through our mouths that we speak, our eyes that we look out on the world, our body attitudes that we sit or stand, and the dynamics with which we move that we express ourselves.

In one course I took with a colleague we had expected an equal number of educationalists and occupational therapists, but at the last minute only two of the latter managed to come. So we had a preponderance of people who had at least had some movement training, and two were lecturers in that subject.

Accordingly we decided to work more on application, the basis of which is making a relationship. One task we gave was to divide in pairs, one partner to enact withdrawal and the other to try and make a contact.

All but one couple achieved their object, and of these the one withdrawn was deliberately determined not to respond whatever happened. As far as I could observe her partner among so many, though doing very interesting movement, playing round the legs of the chair, she appeared to be trying to attract attention rather than to communicate.

All used a silent approach to start with, the majority very quietly and unobtrusively moving around near their partners, so that their presence could be felt, and only when there was some response doing anything further. One "patient" said she had seen feet moving in such a way that she began to feel some confidence in the owner of them. One got through when she used her voice, but her initial approach was to take hold of her "patient" and to try and open her out, which caused a sudden recoil. That was quite instinctive, the "patient" said afterwards that she just couldn't help herself, though she knew the theme and was prepared to co-operate, and obviously had not a patient's difficulties. Only when she heard the voice did she feel the warmth and concern that were present, and then she felt reassured.

These two examples appeared to me to underline the need for greater consciousness and awareness of ourselves as a whole and how we present ourselves to other people.

I wondered whether had the student who had failed been more inwardly involved, or had maybe used her voice, she could have made her presence acceptable in the face of such resistance; and whether had the one who did get through with her voice been able to express herself in her movement as well, she might have avoided the further withdrawal, which in fact increased the difficulties for herself.

QUALITIES NEEDED FOR WORK WITH PATIENTS

In order to be really of service to patients, a person needs to have the basic qualities of warmth, concern and understanding, as well as skills and knowledge; but without the capacity to communicate and relate, these can be of no avail. There is something to be said for the old "bedside manner;" if really genuine it can inspire confidence, and such confidence can produce an attitude in the patient which is in itself an assistance towards healing.

I believe many people desperately desire to be "in touch" with others, but have no idea how to go about it. They shrink from physical touch and are not sufficiently aware of, or secure in, themselves to make any move towards another that is likely to be reciprocated. Their very anxiety is sometimes a barrier.

Great stress is laid today on groups, but just getting people together does not automatically bring relatedness. Some people have a natural aptitude for making friends, others by reason of temperament or conditioning are perhaps gauche, abrupt, remote, affect other people by their attitude and behaviour, and are unable to express their inner states and feelings. Others are just the opposite, and splurge all over everyone until people try and escape whenever they see them coming. All are unaware of the impression they create, or if aware just feel they can do nothing about it.

Sometimes people sense another's reactions, but have no way of relating them to their own approach, or they take all the blame for not being able to make friends with someone, being quite unable to discriminate what lies behind. In emotionally disturbed people everything of this nature becomes exaggerated and they find it so difficult to accept people as they are.

Therefore, in the therapeutic situation, it is all the more important to attempt to establish relationship, even though it may seem the most difficult thing to achieve. Somehow trust and confidence need to be developed.

To refer again to the film "In Touch," the students were shown taking each other's weight in turn, and leading and being led. By experimenting in this interchange of mutual support and reliance on other people we can experience the inner flow of relationship.

THEMES TO DEVELOP TRUST AND CONFIDENCE

Enlarging on these ideas, students may be asked to lean one

against the other, side to side, back to back, one hip against the other's seat, or the back of one against the other's chest. From supporting the partner in a partial way one can take the entire weight of the other (*see* Fig. 20), carrying him on his back or under his arm or across his shoulders. Other ways can be discovered either sitting or lying, one using knees as the support, or a hand and foot, while the other tries out how he can give his weight to that support.

Fig. 20   Taking a partner's weight

Weight can be transferred from one to the other, both sensing the exact moment of transfer and the variation in strength. It is possible to link arms and then see whether another part of the body is required to support the other's weight.

In the film the students, having first worked among themselves, each took a child, and to start with they allowed themselves to be used virtually as a climbing frame, some children being more venturesome than others, the students only giving a helping hand, or changing position to enable the child to explore in safety and security. Sometimes the students swung or lifted the children or let them down to the ground, or balanced them in various ways.

One shot showed a student with a very nervous little girl,

the student lying on her back with her legs bent in the air, the child lying on her lower legs and feet, and finally stretching her arms to balance spreadeagled.

Naturally adults cannot climb about as children do, yet there are many experiments they can make together, adapting their weight to one another.

At first, people find it difficult to let go their weight and allow the partner to take it, or conversely they may find they

Fig. 21 Allowing oneself to be overcome

are not being firm enough to give the other the assurance that he can really give up without being dropped, and therefore it is necessary also to train degrees of strength.

Partners can pit their strength against each other, both exerting to the full, to see if they can hold each other, or one can overcome the other, or one allow himself to be overcome (*see* Fig. 21). They can use increasing and decreasing strength so that they can match their strength, and make great play in the variations achieved.

Leading and being led (*see* Fig. 22) is another theme, using differences in levels, speeds, pathways and touch. The leader learns to trust his own judgment, to make his decisions and to develop reliability whilst at the same time paying attention

105

to his partner, regulating his touch to communicate and extend the range of what he is directing, adjusting as he sees the other gaining confidence. The one being led needs to follow, to submit his will and co-operate with the leader, adapting to what is required of him while being relaxed and yet alert. If he is too tense, he becomes resistant.

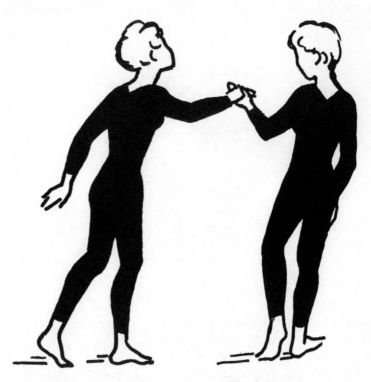

Fig. 22 Leading and following

The same idea can be used with the one following having closed eyes, which requires greater responsibility and sensitivity on the part of the leader, and greater reliance on the leader in the one led. At one point, those being led can be asked to stand still keeping their eyes closed, while the leaders leave their partners and find someone else to lead.

Some people cannot keep their eyes shut, and most of those

106

with whom I have used this theme have found waiting to be picked up a strange experience, one or two even shuddered and said "Horrible," and all were surprised at the differences in the way they were led when their leaders changed.

In such ways, it is possible to train sensitivity and awareness, trust, confidence and responsibility, to give people understanding of what it is like to be dependent, and to stimulate someone to play their part in a relationship. Students need to reverse the roles and play with the ideas in order to learn how to give and also how to take. By conveying consideration and a sense of security they learn how to care for a patient and how to pay attention, so that the other can take and accept the care and help offered.

In all these themes, pliability and flexibility are needed and can be communicated through physical touch to create mutual trust. I hope that it is clear that the touch can range from strong to so delicate that it is barely felt and yet still be meaningful. To develop such fineness of touch people can play with each other's hands and feet (*see* Fig. 23), and

Fig. 23   Playing with hands

gradually relatedness can develop without the need for touch. By the fine adjustments made in leading and following, and in using degrees of weight and strength, sensitivity between people can be found.

I have used such themes not only with therapists and students but also with a few patients. The latter have really been best at "caring for," they can enter into another's feelings by reason of their own difficulties. The problem for them is not to become too involved and identified with the other person's problems. If any help is to be given there must be involvement, but also a certain detachment. One treads a knife-edge between.

Some patients shrink from physical touch, but I have had several become able to bear being touched through playing together in movement, and I believe if touch is used in a sensitive way much can be conveyed that cannot be spoken. Lord Fisher of Lambeth was asked in an interview on the radio about the fact that he so often touched a person's arm or shoulder, etc. and he also maintained that he felt it was important; Dr. Schweizer, going amongst his patients at Lambarene, touched people all the time in gestures of kindliness and greeting. Naturally no-one wants to be mauled about, but people are beginning to realise that touch need not be maudlin or sentimental or an invasion of a person's privacy; in fact with psychotic children it is now thought so necessary that at one place where I worked the children were bathed every night so that they could become aware of others through being handled.

GROUPS AND HOW TO USE THEM

Besides work with partners, there is need to gain experience of groups, to train recognition of the mood of a group, how to handle it, how to get people to work together, when to stimulate and when to calm, when to introduce climax or de-climax. Building to a climax I would use when I desired to get concentration, intensity and generally to stimulate, de-climax when I wanted to produce peace, to quieten and to let emotion die down. When concerned with a single person or only part of a group, it is possible to develop the capacity of having "eyes in the back of one's head," so as to be aware of what is going on elsewhere.

Group sensitivity can also be developed through touch and to this can be added working with the eyes closed. When I was training there was one occasion when we were asked to form a single group, contact one or more people, then close our eyes and wait until we could all start moving in unison. We tried several times but could not get this simultaneous spontaneous co-operation of the whole group; there is a tendency for one person to initiate the start, or for the group to split or pull apart.

The lecturer then had us crouched on the floor in a circle, and chose a student who had to shut her eyes, roll into the middle of the circle, spin herself around so that she didn't know where she was, and then to start moving. When she touched another student, while keeping contact where they had touched, this student also closed her eyes and they moved together until the next one was touched. The lecturer kept four moving together by detaching the first person of each group as the fifth joined in, until all had been involved. At intervals she would ask the four moving to stop, open their eyes and look at the shape they had made together, which was always fascinating. At the completion, we again formed one group and found that we had become so attuned to one another that we could move as a single group. Naturally, all the movement principles and dramatic ideas can be used to help create relationship, but these are specific ways of training people in their approach to patients.

It should not need saying that anyone wanting to work with patients should potentially have certain qualities; it should be realised that if a necessary quality is entirely lacking it cannot be injected, but that latent qualities can be developed. An education lecturer once said to me that a student who wanted to teach must have some ability to keep discipline, and that then it could be developed, but if it were absent they would never be able to learn to keep order. The same is true in the therapeutic field with other qualities, particularly the ability to make a relationship.

Part Four
MUSIC

CHAPTER XI

Response to Music

I HAVE referred previously to the incorporation of music in some rather special ways, now I want to deal with it in more general terms. It certainly plays a very important part both in stimulation and accompaniment. There are people who find music evokes a different response from anything else, and touches them at a profound level.

> One patient wrote: "Some music one always feels one wants to dance to. Sibelius's Symphony No. 2 always makes me want to express my deepest emotions. I feel I want to and must express with the music, the thoughts it arouses in me.
> I dislike all forms of exhibitionism, but the movement to music is not exhibitionism, it is poetry in motion.
> If we can express ourselves in words, by writing, why not express ourselves in movement, free movement to music?"

RECORDED MUSIC

Such music can be extremely useful, either on disc or tape, but then the music dictates the rhythm, phrasing, time and dynamics or quality. By letting themselves be caried by ·the music, some patients can tap unexpected feelings and possibilities in themselves, which may open up a new dimension, or they may get so carried away that primitive feelings may be aroused. These may be experienced and held by the very form and order in the music, or they may become so violent that people are not able to cope with them because of their lack of ego, that part of the individual developed through memory and experience. For those who can suffer such experience, it can be cathartic or abreactive, and can lead to the aggressive tendencies being channelled in the use of the movement.

I'm sure there should be a further state of integration, just "letting off steam" is not sufficient for most people, and it might be that verbalisation with a psychotherapist would be the way in which this could happen.

I was once asked to produce a "War Dance" for some serious schizophrenic patients; I was a bit dubious as I wondered if their violence would burst out. Consequently I chose part of Khachaturian's "Armen Variations" and evolved a dance which was rhythmic, had variety of quality and some dramatic element. I set and taught it, and it went well and was repeated. I used the same dance in another place with less disturbed people and they entered into it with enthusiasm and enjoyed it, except for one girl, who only joined the group when we repeated the dance, as she found it too stirring. There were other reasons as well to explain why she did not come to the movement session again, but I wondered whether, had I known her better, I would have chosen another approach which she and the rest of the group could have accepted.

I have come to think that there are people who, because their aggression is easily triggered off, need to be given music that may evoke a gentler, quieter side of their natures before they can risk anything exciting, in order to have some known, stabilising influence in themselves. This idea occurred to me after watching one girl who, while she improvised, used very flexible, light, delicate movement, and later admitted that to move very freely and express in an aggressive way only aggravated and increased the feelings she couldn't control.

Some people freeze up when music is produced for improvisation and say they cannot do anything, which is quite normal, yet it may be that they are not able to risk "letting go," as they suspect that the music will release the violent, unconscious forces of which they are so afraid, and with good reason.

CHOICE OF MUSIC

In view of all the foregoing, it can be seen that there has

to be discrimination in choice and judicious use of music, particularly when there is more than one person to consider. If one decides beforehand to use certain music for specific movement themes, when the time comes in all probability they will not prove suitable, for the group may be differently constituted, the members have other ideas of their own, or be in quite another mood from that anticipated.

One can, of course, just take a selection of works and let people improvise, and up to a point this is enormously valuable, for one can then provide much variety, from large orchestral works in which the orchestration is magnificent, or choral works with a volume of inspiring sound, to small slow quiet pieces for a few instruments, or similar pianissimo sections in symphonies and oratorios when the restraint of a mass of players or singers can be breathtaking. There is much lighthearted gay music, and as a contrast slow, sustained, even awe-inspiring pieces.

THE IMPORTANCE OF LISTENING IN CHOOSING MUSIC

In choosing music, one has to listen, and this listening demands concentration and judgment which for many people is a real discipline. In these days, we are assailed by background music, and so cease to consider the content unless we set out to pay attention. Similarities in the qualities of music and movement are a good guide. Broadly speaking, they can be equated as follows, and there are probably others.

Movement	Music
Strong/light	Forte/piano. Loud/soft.
Sustained/sudden	Legato/staccato.
	Smooth/detached.
Increase/decrease of speed	Accelerando/ritardando.
Increase/decrease of strength	Crescendo/diminuendo.
Heavily/lightly	Pesante/leggiero.

These are really the basic ingredients of the commonly and probably more acceptable terms used, such as lively, excited, gloomy, sinuous, and so on.

I find if I listen for a variation of volume and speed I can sometimes touch a deeper emotional level, I feel with the

115

music, which may result in the expression of dignity, joy, excitement. Or I may just surge, soar, float, drift or swing in the pure essence or heart of being.

So I would say in listening to music, as in directing movement, that there is a place for the stark simplicity of one or more movement elements. Then no mood or imagery is imposed, but the very fact of the suggestion of crescendo, decrescendo or strength into lightness and dying away leaves the person free to conjure up their own feeling or imagery and can then fulfil the expressive need of the moment, which may have some deep psychological significance for the person concerned, and often develops into dance or drama.

Choice is naturally a very personal matter, but there are one or two rather obvious approaches. One can plan beforehand the movement, dance, or dance drama, and then look for suitable music to accompany; or one can take a work and listen to it, and maybe improvise in movement, to find out what it evokes in images and ideas, and how it affects one both emotionally and physically; or one can listen to the phrasing and the qualities and see if one is stimulated to build and create some movement that will go with them.

One can also look for music for a specific purpose.

1. *Calming and soothing*

Decrease of volume and/or speed. No insistent beat or accent. Quiet, flowing music, or music with a definite form.

Bach	Jesu, Joy of Man's Desiring.
	Air on a **G** String.
Samuel Barber	Adagio for strings.
Brahms	Waltz No. 2.

2. *Stimulating*

Build-up of sound, rhythm or beat, or sudden accent. Climaxes. Exciting, fiery.

Dvořák	Furiant from Slavonic Dances.
Khachaturian	Sabre Dance.

3. *Phrasing*

Flow and pause, as in speaking, a sentence starts and ends,

116

and a breath is taken and leads to a further sentence. Rhythm as distinct from beat.

Dvořák	New World Symphony, 2nd Movement.
	Mazurka from Slavonic Dances, Op. 72.
Debussy	Clair de Lune.

4. *Dramatic*

Music that conjures up an image, a picture, a scene, a situation, conflict, varying moods. Anything that could be mimed or acted.

Holst	The Planets.
Rossini, arranged by *Respighi*	La Boutique fantasque.
Debussy	La Cathédrale Engloutie.

5. *Mime*

Music that suggests definite action.

6. *Formalised, stylised*

Balanced phrasing. Themes and episodes. Repetition. Any of the works of the 18th century, the Dances of *Mozart, Schubert, Grétry, Gluck*, or in the 17th century, of *Praetorius* and *Widman*.

7. *Various moods*, or qualities or basic actions.

Music that changes—quiet to stormy, flowing to staccato.

Brahms	Variations on a theme of Handel.
Oram and Lasry-Baschet	Electronic music.
Elgar	Enigma Variations.

8. *Gay, light-hearted*

Music that is lively, rhythmical, perhaps a dotted rhythm, or quick and light, accented.

Brahms	Some of the waltzes.
Smetana	Dances.
Kabalevsky	Dances.
Mozart	Dances.

117

These are only some examples, and suggestions of where to look for suitable passages for what one wants. The choice is purely personal, in fact I myself might feel at times that though I have used music under the category mentioned and found it satisfactory, at another time I might either want to use the music quite differently or feel it no longer fitted the mood I had used it for previously.

The only way is to try for oneself, and depend on one's own judgment. Usually it is only a part of a work that is suitable, and then one has to decide whether it can be used separately. At times, it is necessary to be able to hear a distinct beginning and an end. The need is to *listen*, and these are only ideas of how to go about it. Record libraries are invaluable, and many public libraries have a record lending department.

CHAPTER XII

Music as Therapy

CONSIDERATION OF GROUP PREFERENCES

BESIDES making one's own choice there are other considerations: the individual likes or dislikes of the group. Some do not like recorded music, and others do not like an accompanist. Some will only join in if they are free to do anything they like. Others say: "I like to be told what to do." Sometimes, one can get round this by using music for which one has prepared a theme, but say that those who want to be on their own can disregard any directions. For this reason, it is advisable to have several contrasting ideas and music in order to strike a balance between all the fancies of the group, and to give each person a chance to have a satisfying, creative experience. At the same time, one can expect them to join in with others and adapt to the situation to a certain extent.

1. *The value of having an accompanist*

If one can have a sympathetic accompanist, then catering for all these differences is much easier. But one needs a pianist who can improvise and enter into the requirements in such a way that they are really participating in the work and the general mood. If they can also sight-read and play set music it is marvellous. I have been blessed with two patients who were able to improvise in this way.

Such pianists can suit the music to the need of the moment, they can follow what people are doing, and change the music according to what emerges, or they can create an accompaniment to a movement sequence or dance. They can take the lead and improvise the type of music that will stimulate a mood, for instance, something quick and lively to get activity,

119

or movement all about the room. Or they may produce something fluid, quiet and flowing, which may have a calming effect or evoke flexibility or flow. They can use climax and de-climax according to whether the group needs to have something exciting or something to capture their interest, or whether they need relaxing or "letting-go" so that their energy can be reduced.

There is a feeling of achievement if the group either individually or together invent a movement sequence or a dance for which the accompanist composes the music with them. There is great satisfaction in such corporate activity, the whole being completed by the mutual co-operation and contribution of each individual, so that they feel it is entirely of their own making. There is also the extraordinary moment when the dancer and accompanist are imagining and accompanying each other, producing a peak of intuitive agreement.

The piano is, however, a limited instrument in that it is basically percussive, and we often need sustained sound such as can be played on string or wind instruments. For the majority of us, this means recorded music again.

2. *Use of percussion*

Sometimes, members of the group can use percussion as an accompaniment, either with or without the accompanist playing the piano. Patients usually find this very difficult and are inclined to bang out a regular beat without any liveliness, accent or variation. If they can explore the different sounds they can get out of an instrument, and then get together and see what they can invent, they find that they can stimulate each other in many different ways.

There are times when one has to make do without any music—no accompanist, no record-player, perhaps a tape-recorder which only plays one speed which is different from the recordings one has. I have been faced with this situation quite unexpectedly, but it doesn't really matter. In fact, I do a great deal of work without music. I find that people so often have never had the opportunity of discovering their own rhythm, and working without music they can go at their own speed, and really establish how they themselves would do a movement. We often talk about rhythm in painting, and there

120

is rhythm in speech. So we can rely on the natural rhythm in ourselves. When I have agreed to take a class of under-fives I have found that they will work happily without music, in fact often if I put on a record, they will completely ignore it and each will carry on in his own way. After all, they are at different stages of development even if they are the same age; they are different in weight, size, and shape, which all influences rhythm. Normal young children also cannot listen to long sentences of sound, they need "noises," percussive and elongated sound.

THE USE OF VOICE

Even without music, one has a voice and one can easily accompany or stimulate with it. We all have hands, so it is possible to clap, and the clapping can be done on different parts of the body, on the floor, on different surfaces. If one wants anything further, many things will function as a percussion instrument—a plastic bucket makes a handy drum, pins or nails in a tin can make a rattle, and I have known someone use the tools from her car suspended on a stick, which made sounds at different pitches so that one could play a tune. One can use the phrasing of breathing as a basis for rhythm or one can feel the heartbeat and walk to that. Laban used the former for arm gestures, and the latter for locomotion.

Nevertheless, music enhances and enriches the experience of a movement session, and there is an enormous amount to choose from. In fact, it is sometimes bewildering to know what to use out of all that is possible.

APPENDIX I

General List of Useful Musical Pieces

Albéniz	Tango.
Arnold, Malcolm	English Dances.
Bach, J. S.	Brandenburg Concertos.
	Sleepers' Wake.
	Choral Preludes.
	Jesu, Joy of Man's Desiring.
Barber, Samuel	Adagio for Strings.
Bartók	Children's Pieces.
	Roumanian Folk Songs.
Benjamin, Arthur	Rumba.
	Matti Rag.
	Caribbean.
Bizet	Carmen.
Bloch, Ernest	Concerto Grossi 1 and 2.
Brahms	Waltzes.
	Hungarian Dances.
	Variations on a theme by Handel.
	Variations on a theme by Haydn.
	Double Concerto.
Britten, Benjamin	Young Person's Guide to the Orchestra.
Carmichael	Bahama Rumba.
Clarke, Jeremiah	Trumpet Voluntary.
Copland, Aaron	Appalachian Spring.
	Rodeo.
Debussy	Various Piano Pieces.
Elgar	Enigma Variations.
Davies, Walford	Solemn Melody.

Delibes	Coppélia.
	Discord and War.
Don Gillis	5½ Symphony.
Dukas	Sorcerer's Appentice.
Dvořák	Slavonic Dances.
	New World Symphony.
	Symphony No. 8.
	Piano Quintet.
Fauré	Pelléas et Mélisande.
	Dolly (Suite).
Glazunov	Seasons.
Gluck	Ballet Suite Iphigenia in Aulis.
Grétry	Céphale et Procris.
Handel	Water Music.
Heynssen, Adda	Music for Modern Dance (Published by Macdonald & Evans Ltd., 8 John Street, London WC1N 2HY).
Holst, Gustav	The Planets.
	Brook Green Suite
	The Perfect Fool (Ballet music).
Janáček	Praeludium.
	Lach Dances.
Kabalevsky	Dances.
Khachaturian	Gayaneh Suite.
Kodály	Háry János.
Lambert, Constant	The Rio Grande.
Lasry-Baschet	Electronic music.
Litolff	Concerto Symphonique.
Milhaud	Suite provençale.
	Saudades do Brazil.
	Scaramouche.
Mozart	Dances.
	Eine Kleine Nachtmusik.
	Horn Concertos Nos. 3 and 4.
Moszkowski	Spanish Waltzes.
Mussorgsky	Scherzo.
	Scorotchinska Fair.
Nielsen	Petite Suite for Strings.
Offenbach	Can-can from "Orpheus in the Underworld."

Oram	Electronic music.
Poulenc	Les Biches.
	Clarinet Concerto.
	Oboe Concerto.
	Sonata for two Pianos.
Praetorius and Widman	Dances from "Terpsichore."
Prokofiev	Lieutenant Kijé.
	Classical Symphony.
Rachmaninov	Symphonic Dances.
	Rhapsody on a theme of Paganini.
Ravel	Mother Goose Suite.
	Boléro.
	Pavane pour une infante Defunte.
	Daphnis et Chlöe.
Rimsky-Korsakov	Cappriccio Espagnole.
Rossini	Cat Duet.
Satie	Trois Gymnopédies.
	Les Trois Valses.
	Avant-dernières pensées.
	Trois Gnossiennes.
Schubert	Variations in A Flat Major.
	Fantasy in F Minor.
	Piano Quintet.
	Dances.
	Marches.
Schumann	Kinderscenen.
	Études symphoniques.
	Papillons.
Shostakovitch	Fantastic Dances.
Smetana	Dances.
Strauss	Dances.
	Accelerando Waltz.
Stravinsky	Circus Polka.
Tchaikovsky	Nutcracker Suite.
	Andante Cantabile from String Quartet No. 1 in D Major.
Vivaldi	The Four Seasons.
Wagner	Overtures.
Warlock, Peter	Capriol Suite.

APPENDIX II

Bibliography

BOOKS

Bertine, Eleanor. *Human Relations*, Longman Green & Co., 1958.

Boom, Alfred, ed. *Studies on the Mentally-Handicapped Child*, Edward Arnold, 1968.

Fordham, Frieda. *An Introduction to Jung's Psychology*, Penguin Books, 1953.

Jung, C. G. *Modern Man in Search of a Soul*, Routledge and Kegan Paul, 1933.

Jung, C. G. *Collected Works*, Volume 10, Routledge and Kegan Paul, 1964.

Laban, Rudolf. *The Mastery of Movement*, Macdonald and Evans, Ltd., Third edition, 1971.

Laban, Rudolf. *Modern Educational Dance*, Macdonald and Evans, Ltd., Second edition, 1968.

Lamb, Warren. *Posture and Gesture*, Duckworth, 1965.

Lyddiatt, E. M. *Spontaneous Painting and Modelling*, Constable, 1970.

Ogden, C. K., ed. Science Editions Series, Routledge and Kegan Paul, 1950.

Reitman, Dr. F. *Psychotic Art*, Routledge and Kegan Paul, 1950.

Russell, Joan. *Creative Dance in the Primary School*, Macdonald and Evans, Ltd., 1965.

Russell, Joan. *Creative Dance in the Secondary School*, Macdonald and Evans, Ltd., 1969.

Russell, Joan. *Modern Dance in Education*, Macdonald and Evans, Ltd., 1958.

Schilder, P. *The Image and Appearance of the Human Body*, Routledge and Kegan Paul, 1925.

Slade, Peter. *An Introduction to Child Drama*, University of London Press, 1958.

Slade, Peter. *Child Drama*, University of London Press, 1954.
Slade, Peter. *Experience of Spontaneity*, Longman, 1968.
Sorell, Walter, ed. *The Dance has Many Faces*, Columbia, 1966.
Stanislavski, Constantin. *Stanislavski's Legacy*, ed. and trans. E. Hapgood, Bodley Head, 1968.
Storr, Anthony, *The Integrity of the Personality*, Heinemann, 1969.
Thornton, S. *A Movement Perspective of Rudolf Laban*, Macdonald and Evans, Ltd., 1971.
Ullmann, Lisa, ed. and selected. *Rudolf Laban Speaks About Movement*, Laban Art of Movement Centre, Addlestone, Surrey.

ARTICLES

*Bartenieff, Irmgard. *How is the Dancing Teacher Equipped to do Dance Therapy?* (March 1958, No. 20).
Champernowne, Irene. *Art and Therapy. An Uneasy Partnership* (Inscape. Journal of the British Association of Art Therapists No. 3, 1971).
*Collingden and Gardner. *The Arts in Therapy* (March 1956, No. 16).
*Davis, Diana. *Movement Therapy* (May 1966, No. 36).
*Gardner, Chloë. *My Experience of Teaching Movement to Psychiatric Cases* (May 1965, No. 34).
*Goodall, Ken. *Making Friends With Schizophrenics* (May 1965, No. 34).
*Lamb, Warren. *Recruiting and Assessing from the Evidence of Movement* (November 1966, No. 37).
*Meredith Jones, B. *Moving and Living. Elderly People* (May 1961, No. 27).
*Sherborne, Veronica. *Report on Lecture at Conference* (Easter 1965).
*Wethered, Audrey. *Movement and Personality Difficulties* (November 1958, No. 21).
*Wethered, Audrey. *Movement Therapy in a Residential Psychotheraputic Setting* (May 1965, No. 34).
Wethered, Audrey. *The Enigmatic Oneness of the Living Being* Journal of the Analytical Psychology Club (1965, No. 11).

*Laban Art of Movement Guild Magazine.

INDEX

BODY AWARENESS:
  Body image, 32, 36, 50
  Exploration by infant, 31–3, 35
  Instrument of action, expression and communication, 3, 9, 10, 33
  Preparation of body for action, 18–21
  Use of isolated parts, 19, 98, 99
  What we move, 3, 4

CHARACTERSTIC BODY ATTITUDE AND MOVEMENT:
  Contracted or neutralised, 21, 36
  Folded in, 21, 36, 37
  Repetitive, 37, 55, 56, 62
  Shuffling, 21, 55
  Swaying, rocking, 37

COMMUNICATION:
  Body, instrument of, 9, 101
  Speech, 72, 74, 102
  Through singing and touch, 52–4
  Voice, 45, 54, 102

CONCENTRATION, 62, 66, 81, 82, 96

CREATION, see Improvisation

FANTASY:
  Body image, 50
  Dim light, 82
  Dissociation, 46
  Pattern in, 47–9
  Relating to actuality, 49
  Starting point, 49

GROUPS:
  Advantages and difficulties of, 61–5
  Difficulty for some people, 36
  Drama groups, Holyrood, 66–78
  Drama groups, Sesame, 79–87
  General work and handling, 81–3
  Getting together, 103
  Goodmayes Hospital, 83–7
  Interplay, 61, 62

IMPROVISATION AND CREATION:
  Child's joy in creating, 33
  Goodmayes Hospital, 70–87
  Holyrood, 66–78
  Improvisation to music, 43, 54, 113
  Improvising scene or mime, 67, 70, 83
  "Spontaneous acting," 63, 67
  Work with groups, 53, 63, 67, 70, 76, 77, 117, 118
  Writing a play, 64

LIMBER-UP:
  Preparing body for action, 18
  Starting, 62
  Various ways, 19–21

MOVEMENT:
  Related to objects, 38, 41, 49, 51
  Related to painting, 38, 49

MUSIC:
  Accompanist, 119
  Choosing music, 114–19
  Effect on people, 113, 114
  Group improvisation, 53
  Improvising movement to music, 43, 54, 113, 114, 115
  Listening, 52, 53, 115, 116, 118
  Music for specific purposes, 116–18
  Percussion, 53, 54, 120
  Rhythm, 21, 52, 54, 120, 121
  Using piano technique, 51, 52

OBSERVATION:
  Laxity in observing, 71
  Necessity of observation in order to understand, 12, 17, 31, 36, 81, 82
  We all observe, 9, 10

PERSONALITY:
  The "whole" person, 56
  Uniqueness revealed in movement, 11, 12

PLAY:
Adults and play, 34
Missed in childhood, 31, 33
Personal and projected, 32

PRINCIPLES OF MOVEMENT; *see* Body
awareness, Space, Quality, Relationship
Used in therapy, 30 ff.

QUALITY:
Basic actions, 12–15
Elements or motion factors, 8, 11–12,
41–6, 55, 56, 57, 107
Elements used in mime, 17
Expression of inner states, 12
Movement qualities: Energy, Space,
Time, Flow, 10–12
Variations in speed and volume,
15, 16

RELATIONSHIP (FLOW):
Concerted action, 71, 72
Development of trust and confidence,
103–8
Give and take, 63
Group sensitivity, 109
How do we relate, communicate and
respond? 100–3
Patients' difficulties, 62
Relation to the outside world, 63
With whom we move, 4
Working out hostility, 76

RELAXATION AND TENSION:
Using a piano, 51, 52
Ways of achieving relaxation, 91–8

RHYTHM, 21, 52, 54, 120, 121

SHAPE:
Body shape, 4
Floor pattern, 57
Pathways, 9
Pattern, 47–9

SPACE:
Area in which working, 38
Dimensions and diagonals, 6–8
Expansion and contraction, 8
Exploring space, 37, 38
How we move into space, 11, 13
Levels, 58
Pattern, 49
Personal and general, 89

THE THERAPIST:
"Holding the ring," 44
Preparing work, 17, 79
Role of the therapist, x, xi
Therapeutic team, 56
What is needed in a therapist? x, xi,
44, 102, 103

TOUCH:
Piano, 51, 52
Recoil from, 33, 49, 51, 102
Training trust and confidence, 103–9

VARIETY OF ABILITY, 62, 79

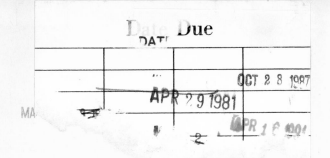